"With a clear and thoughtful voice, Candace V. Love describes, through relevant case examples, how to identify and discern important self-defeating versus self-supportive life patterns; providing effective methods for forging a compassionate bond with the vulnerable side of ourselves in order to steer clear of narcissistic seduction and to achieve healthy, reciprocally balanced, needs-meeting relationships. This book will surely bring added value to your personal library."

—**Wendy T. Behary, LCSW**, author of *Disarming the Narcissist*

"This is the book for women who are wondering *Was it him or was it me?* The answer is here; not whose fault it was, but what actually happened, and solid psychological advice about how to keep it from happening again."

—**Albert J. Bernstein PhD**, author of *Dinosaur Brains* and *Emotional Vampires*

"Candace V. Love has written a marvelously accessible and interesting book for women seeking to understand how to change chronic patterns that have resulted in toxic relationships with narcissistic men. Her book offers insightful self-assessment tools and many effective strategies for healing and growing and, last but not least, for de ing the art and skill of relationship wisdom."

—**Eleanor Payson, LMSW**, auth *and Other Narcissists*

"The first step in making posi to identify the source of your suffering. *No More Narcissis* help you understand how your core beliefs and their related patterns of behavior, including partner selection, have kept you stuck in romantic relationships that are damaging to you."

—**Michelle Skeen, PsyD**, author of *Love Me, Don't Leave Me*

"Required reading for anyone romantically involved with a narcissist! Built upon proven psychological research and delivered in an engaging and readable style, this book is chock-full of insights and exercises for the reader. Candace V. Love is a relationship guru and BFF all rolled up into one; walking with you arm-in-arm and skillfully guiding you through the intricacies and entrapments of your narcissistic relationship."

> —**Neil J. Lavender, PhD**, licensed psychologist, professor
> of psychology at Ocean County College in New Jersey,
> and coauthor of *The One-Way Relationship Workbook* and
> *Impossible to Please*

No More Narcissists!

How to Stop Choosing Self-Absorbed Men *and* Find the Love You Deserve

CANDACE V. LOVE, PhD

New Harbinger Publications, Inc.

Publisher's Note

Distributed in Canada by Raincoast Books

Copyright © 2016 by Candace V. Love
        New Harbinger Publications, Inc.
        5674 Shattuck Avenue
        Oakland, CA 94609
        www.newharbinger.com

Cover design by Sara Christian
Acquired by Melissa Valentine
Edited by Jean Blomquist

Library of Congress Cataloging-in-Publication Data on file

Printed in the United States of America

18   17   16

10   9   8   7   6   5   4   3   2   1   First printing

To my mentor Barbara Gerbert, PhD, who gave me
the opportunity to transform my life

In memory of my friend
Jean Walker, MD

To my parents,
Gust and Marie Melonas

Contents

Introduction 1

1   Prince Charming or Another Frog? 9

2   The Frog: Understanding Narcissism and Narcissists 27

3   Unmet Childhood Needs: Discovering Your Story 53

4   A Closer Look at Life Traps 63

5   Stuck for Life? Your Life Traps in Adulthood 87

6   Learn to Change Your Life Traps 121

7   Self-Care: Becoming Your Own Fairy Godmother 151

8   Mindful Dating 179

A Few Last Thoughts... 199

Acknowledgments 201

Appendix: List of Exercises 203

Notes 207

References 209

Introduction

If you are one of the many women who find yourself in one toxic, destructive relationship after another and can't understand why your relationships implode, the problem may be that you are picking one self-absorbed, self-serving narcissistic partner after another. What's worse is that you don't even realize you're doing it. Well, I have good news for you. You can learn to stop repeating this destructive relationship pattern. As a clinical psychologist, I have helped many women like you break this pattern. This book is for you and the many women like you who struggle with this issue. One such woman is Linda. See if her story sounds familiar.

Linda's Story

Sitting alone at the bar of a trendy restaurant, Linda squeezed the stem of her wine glass tightly. Her stomach had that scooped-out feeling of loss, and she could feel the weight of sadness building up in her throat. *Stop. Not yet. I don't want to start crying now.* She checked the time on her smartphone…again. Nancy was always late. Nancy had been her closest friend since childhood, and Linda really needed to talk to her. Linda thought back to the time when she and Nancy had their first hot yoga class a few years earlier, and she had told Nancy about her latest boyfriend, Marc. Things seemed so hopeful then, and Linda began to daydream, remembering how happy she had felt in the beginning of her relationship with Marc. While Linda daydreamed, Nancy finally arrived. Ignoring the attempts of the hostess to seat her, Nancy headed directly for Linda at the bar.

They hugged, and as they walked from the bar to a table, Nancy said how sorry she was to hear about Linda's breakup. Once they sat down, Linda took a breath and said quietly, "I can't believe it happened again. I really thought he was different. How can this be happening to me? What did I miss?" Linda proceeded to unload the painful details, finally coming clean as to just how bad things had gotten between her and Marc. He had become increasingly irritable, starting fights over the littlest things. His insults were filled with contempt as he became more demanding and critical of her. She couldn't do anything right. Then, when she found out that he had gone out with a woman from his office, she felt sure he had slept with her. Linda remembered how he had followed the woman around like a puppy, flirting with her at the Christmas party. He denied it, of course, and accused Linda of being a typical jealous woman.

As she spoke, Linda fought to keep her thoughts rational but felt them sinking into the familiar whirlpool of shame. *I'm an idiot! Something is really wrong with me. I keep screwing up! I should have known better. This is so embarrassing. Oh, my God, I'm hopeless. I should just give up trying to find someone. I'm going to be alone the rest of my life.*

Nancy looked at the small mound of shredded paper napkin bits that Linda had created while she talked. "Linda," Nancy said, taking her hand, "I didn't know it was this bad. You know what I went through a couple years ago with David. I wish you had told me. You didn't have to go through this alone." Linda looked up, her eyes misty with the tears she had been trying to hold back. "I couldn't… I couldn't even say it to myself. I felt so ashamed when I realized I was in yet another loser relationship. I didn't want to admit it," Linda murmured. Nancy gave her hand a squeeze.

Maybe you can relate to Linda. Maybe you, too, have been through countless relationships that start out looking and feeling *so right* but inevitably turn bitter with disappointment. You are not alone if you find you continue to attract and be attracted to narcissistic men. (I'll explain exactly what a narcissist is in chapter 2.) The fact is many women repeat the same self-destructive patterns in their relationships. If you are one of the unlucky ones who do, you probably feel frustrated and angry with yourself for not seeing the truth of the relationship sooner, or for not leaving sooner. You may be filled with tremendous shame that you allowed yourself to be fooled and/or mistreated. You may feel guilty that you subjected others, such as your children or a dependent parent, to him. You may feel like you wasted precious time in another dead-end relationship. Or perhaps because you were hoping to marry and start a family before your childbearing years were over or because your marriage of many years ended, you may feel you wasted the best years of your life with this man.

Repeating these patterns leaves you feeling deeply wounded and flawed. Your self-confidence is severely shaken, and your self-esteem seriously eroded. You are filled with shame that you, yet again, failed in a relationship. These types of soul-shattering relationships shake you to the core: you believe you cannot trust your judgment. Going forward, you may decide to avoid relationships altogether, though you've always hoped to share your life with someone. What is the problem?

The problem is that narcissistic partners can initially seem so appealing that it can be hard for those involved with them to break away. These men can be charming and caring in the beginning. They seem to be on top of their game and have it all: confident and with a magnetic attractiveness. They make you feel special because they chose you. You happily and easily slip into their life. You can't believe how lucky you are. Now you won't be alone the rest of your life. You're going to have a golden relationship. But then it changes, as it always does and will.

Your Prince Charming begins critiquing every little thing you do—from how you dress and wear your hair to how you talk, from your intellect to your friends and family; on and on the list goes. You begin to get nervous. What's happening? Fear sets in as you realize you may lose him because you aren't measuring up to his expectations—and then self-doubt: How could you have thought you could hold on to him? He is so great and you are, well...you. And you know you are not that special. The relationship dissolves in front of you. Either he drops you out of the blue, or you end it because you have no other choice. You lick your wounds, your girlfriends and family tell you they never liked him anyway, and in time you meet another man. And it starts over again. You don't intend to, but you find yourself in another bad relationship. Unwittingly, you keep picking a man who can't give you the love you desire.

Because of the unfortunate psychology of narcissists, they are actually unable to love another person in a way that is deep, reciprocal, mutually respectful, and satisfying. Narcissistic men are self-absorbed and can never really love or appreciate you. They only love and appreciate what you do for them—the way you look, your status, or your service to them. Focused solely on fulfilling their own needs, narcissistic men are unable to perceive things from another person's perspective or to relate to a partner with kindness, respect, and sensitivity.

To keep yourself from entering into these unhealthy relationships, you have to stop focusing on other people's wants and needs and begin focusing on you. What is it about you that causes you to be attracted to these men and to stay way too long in hurtful, destructive relationships?

It's not the man who has to change. It's *you*. You do it by learning about the psychological patterns you developed in childhood as a result of your unmet childhood needs, such as nurturance, empathy, love, security, and safety. These unmet needs develop into unhealthy patterns of behavior that become an unconscious prism through which you view and respond to the world around you. They tend to persist throughout your life, causing you to look in the wrong places or to the wrong people to fulfill them. They most certainly impact your dating choices unless you consciously identify and change them. I want to help you change.

I wrote this book because I have a passion—no, a *mission*—to help smart women like you who keep finding themselves, yet again, with another jerk—a narcissist, to be precise. I want to help you learn how to stop repeating those destructive relationships. I feel a lot of empathy for women like you because I, too, was a smart woman (heck, a clinical psychologist, for God's sake) who kept repeating narcissistic relationships. I finally had to accept that I was the common denominator in these unhealthy and oftentimes damaging relationships. I went through the self-blame and shame of having been dead wrong about someone who seemed like a great guy in the beginning, at least to me. Friends, of course, saw things otherwise, but I didn't listen to them. Instead I would say to myself the classic phrase, *They don't know him like I do.* Yeah, right, infamous last words. Then the relationship inevitably came back to bite me in the derrière. Who knew that by disagreeing or displeasing a narcissist he would morph from Prince Charming into a cold, detached komodo dragon intent on destroying me? It left me feeling like I'd been the victim of a drive-by shooting. Even though I was the one who ended these relationships, I still felt shocked and confused. Then I would interrogate myself: *What just happened? What did I miss? How could I have missed it? What's wrong with me? I am an idiot!* I was left in a wake of trauma, flailing in a sea of doubt and self-recrimination, as the supposed man of my dreams raced away in a speedboat—classic, sleek, and expensive, of course—never looking back.

I have to admit, I have always been attracted to narcissists. What's not to be attracted to? They are usually funny, witty, intelligent guys with larger-than-life personalities who are seemingly confident, often success-ful, and in control. And, initially, they make me feel safe and special. But the pattern is always the same. What I took to be ardent love was actually the need to control me, and in a couple cases when I displeased them, disagreed with them, or just offered up my own voice, God forbid, they became vindictive and very scary. But my illusions and need to hold on to the fantasy of what I wanted them to be was powerful. I remember declar-ing to one such scary narcissist after dating for only a few months, "This is the healthiest relationship I have ever been in." Can you imagine? Boy, did I ever have to eat those words—and with a helping of habanero peppers!

So my promise to you is that, if you follow the wisdom offered in this book—wisdom gained from my own painful experiences as well as those of countless women I have worked with—you can break this pattern once and for all. The theoretical basis for the teachings in this book is schema therapy, developed by renowned American psychologist Jeffrey Young.[1] Schema therapy is a powerful, effective approach to changing unhealthy behaviors. Schemas, called *life traps* in this book, are the unconscious pat-terns developed in childhood and carried into adulthood that drive you toward destructive relationships and hold you captive, even when you know better. As adults, we tend to be drawn to people who trigger our particular unconscious patterns, or life traps, because they feel familiar to us. Women who are attracted to narcissistic men tend to have inherited the specific life traps of abandonment, mistrust/abuse, emotional depriva-tion, defectiveness/shame, subjugation, self-sacrifice, and unrelenting standards. With this book, you will learn to identify your particular life traps and break your pattern of repeatedly getting involved with narcis-sistic men.

I strongly suggest that you read this book straight through rather than skip around. I designed it so that the information and skills offered build on each other. The book is also meant to be interactive, so try not to be a passive reader. If you are, you will miss a lot. Making lasting changes in your behavior requires practice and commitment. If you just read the book without participating, you will not get the full benefit, which is for you to stop repeating narcissistic relationships.

No More Narcissists! begins with an overview of why you have been attracted to narcissists by explaining about schema theory and unmet childhood needs that followed you into adulthood (chapter 1). It explains narcissism and narcissistic relationships (chapter 2). Then you will identify your life traps and learn how to change them using basic building blocks of change (chapters 3–6). To help heal your wounds from childhood and destructive relationships, you will learn the importance of self-care (chapter 7). And lastly, you will put this all together as you learn how to date successfully (chapter 8).

Each chapter includes some common elements. Throughout the book, you'll find composite stories based on women I have worked with. Each chapter provides a preview of essential elements presented in the chapter along with a sprinkling of targeted exercises and techniques. Occasionally, I will ask you to check in with how you are feeling and ask you to reflect on what you just read. Increasing your awareness is the first step to changing your behavior. Developing the habit of reflecting on your thoughts and feelings will also serve you well when you date a new man. I call this "Your Looking Glass," just like the mirror often used in fairy tales to seek out truth.

You will get the most out of this book if you keep a journal to record your journey as you work your way through it. I recommend a three-ring binder or something similar so you can flip back and see your progress.

I want you to know that you don't have to give up on your happy ending. You no longer have to be trapped by your unmet childhood needs. Through the step-by-step process I present here, you will identify your life traps, learn the influence they have had on your choice of men, and develop the skills necessary to change so that not only will you never experience another destructive relationship, but you will also increase your chance of finding the loving partner and relationship you desperately desire.

By the time you have finished reading *No More Narcissists!*, you will realize that being attracted to narcissistic men has *never* been your fault. The way you have come to view yourself and the world is the result of things that happened to you in your childhood—things that were beyond your control. *This* is what has trapped you into repeating unhealthy relationships. You can change once you understand that you have more control than you realize, not over others but over your own responses. In essence, you will learn to become your own fairy godmother (more on this in chapters 1 and 7) and create your own happily-ever-after with a healthy Prince Charming. It doesn't happen overnight, but if you are committed to the process and have patience and courage to follow the steps offered in this book, you are much more likely to find love that is true and lasting.

CHAPTER 1

Prince Charming or Another Frog?

Shortly after she completed medical school, Jessica met Todd. Brilliant, sexy, and successful, Todd swept Jessica off her feet. She was attracted to him immediately, and during their first few weeks together, his lavish compliments and loving attention made her feel special—and secure. He often told her, "I just can't get enough of you!" Best of all, her mom loved Todd. Gaining her mother's approval was rare, not only when it came to boyfriends but also in every aspect of Jessica's life, so Todd appeared to be the perfect partner.

As a single woman just starting out as a first-year medical doctor, she was finally making a decent income, but her father had lost his job, and Jessica felt obligated to help support her parents. This cut into her own financial goal of buying her first condo. If she married Todd, there would be two incomes, and she would be able to take care of her parents' needs as well as her own.

But after the glow of their initial time together, Jessica and Todd's fairy-tale relationship turned dark. Todd began making snide remarks about Jessica's habits, flaws, and personality. These soon escalated into verbal abuse. Todd lashed out, telling her she was fat and boring. If she didn't agree with him about something, he became angry, yelling and intimidating her. What's worse, he never took responsibility for his actions, shrugging off any hurt he had inflicted. If he was caught in a lie or proven wrong about something, he played the victim. His demeanor took on an icy coldness, unlike his initial charming persona. When Jessica told him of her successes at work, he offered no support or congratulations. It seemed he simply couldn't be happy for her or anyone else's success. When they were out with friends, he monopolized conversations and cut her and others off. It was all about him, all about Todd.

At first, Jessica was shocked. She couldn't believe that her affectionate Prince Charming—the guy who'd initially rushed her into meeting his family and professed to be "family oriented"—could turn into such a nasty adversary. Maybe it was her. Maybe there was some truth to his criticism and accusations. Not wanting to face the truth that their relationship was not the one she hoped it would be, she tried to either ignore or rationalize Todd's malicious attacks, but when she could no longer hide from the truth, she became confused and frightened. How had Todd changed so drastically from the guy she'd originally fallen for? Was this just a bad spell? She worried that losing Todd meant that again she'd be alone and unhappy, struggling with the burden of financially caring for her parents. She fantasized that Todd would treat her better after they were married and that perhaps it was just a fear of commitment that caused him to act out. So she stuck it out. When Todd asked her to marry him a couple of years later, Jessica was hopeful and also relieved that being married would help with her financial stress. But after three miserable years of desperately trying to hang on to her marriage, she ended the relationship. Jessica was heartbroken. She was sure it was her fault and could "just feel" her mother's tacit agreement.

Within a year, Jessica met Ethan. She was well aware that his stellar attributes easily measured up to Jessica's mother's standards: successful, smart, rich. But after a few weeks of romantic dinners and blissful sex, Ethan's disapproving nature emerged. "Why do you wear clothes that are so unflattering? And your hairstyle is so…unhip. You should go to a better salon." Ethan got more specific in his demands: Jessica should dress sexier and trendier; wear shorter, tighter skirts and higher heels. Jessica's appearance wasn't the only thing that needed a makeover; Ethan also wanted her to focus on certain topics when they were out with his friends. As for her friends, they weren't interesting or sophisticated enough for him. And he didn't like her family either. In other words, in almost every department (except for sex), Jessica didn't fulfill Ethan's requirements for an acceptable girlfriend. Never mind that she was kind, thoughtful, and highly educated, or that she had been invited to join the staff and faculty at the city's premier hospital. Jessica didn't fit Ethan's exacting criteria.

Despite the red flags, Jessica was desperate to hold on to Ethan. And in spite of all of his criticisms, she was thrilled beyond belief when he planned a trip to Venice for them and e-mailed her telling her about the three-plus-carat diamond engagement ring he was buying for her. Needless to say, Jessica was floored when later that week Ethan broke up with her— via a text. His text informed Jessica that he was putting her things in a brown paper bag and would be leaving them with the doorman of her apartment building. Jessica was in total shock. She had no idea anything had been wrong. Ethan's change of heart seemed to have come out of the blue. Her self-confidence was shattered.

Todd and Ethan were just two of the narcissistic partners Jessica was involved with when she was in her twenties. There were others. Was there something about Jessica that was a magnet for narcissistic guys? Or was there something about them that drew her in? It wasn't until Jessica explored her family's psychological dynamic and its influence on her relationships with men that she came to understand why she was habitually drawn to men who were narcissists, and why they were attracted to her.

Jessica's story reflects her wish for a fairy-tale romance where her Prince Charming would sweep her off her feet and fix all her problems. She was blindsided by her unmet needs and desires, and could not see the real man behind the fairy tale she wanted to believe in. Her "forever after" ended the only way it could because the spell of her unmet needs and desires was cast long ago when she was still a child. It set up a pattern of being attracted to narcissistic men and only seeing what she wanted to see—a pattern Jessica was now trapped in repeating.

Jessica's story illustrates how dangerous it can be to be blind to the patterns that trap us into repeating unhealthy, destructive relationships and leave us vulnerable to the dark side of a supposed Prince Charming. The result can be a broken heart again…and again…and again.

We've All Been There: Our Struggle to Find the Happily-Ever-After

Does Jessica's struggle to find a "happily ever after" relationship sound familiar? Have you been through the aftermath of yet another destructive relationship? Have you had those same feelings or thoughts as Jessica? I've heard this same story many times in the privacy of my office. Each "Jessica" has tried in earnest many times to find the love of her life, only to discover herself in yet another failed relationship and with the feeling of being ready to give up. It must be *her* that doesn't work. After all, she is the common denominator in all these failed relationships. The sense of shame associated with this type of repeated loss becomes unbearable. You may ask yourself, *What's wrong with me?* or, feeling hopeless and defeated, you may wonder, *Why should I put myself through this again?* Eventually, you think, *Perhaps the dream of a loving partner or husband and a family has been just that—a dream—at least for me.*

I want you to know that there is hope and help for you to change this pattern of failed relationships. Really! I know you're thinking, *Yeah right, this won't really work.* Actually, it *will* work. I didn't write just another self-help book that tells you about the problem but doesn't offer real solutions or the tools and skills to help you change. I'm not offering a quick fix, but I am offering you the chance for a healthy relationship, one you can build a future on. You just need to suspend judgment and try. As you read, you will come to understand how experiences from your childhood and adolescence have trapped you into repeating unhealthy patterns of behavior. Using the skill-building tools offered here can set you free from repeating unhealthy, narcissistic relationships.

Essential Elements

In this chapter, we'll explore the reasons why narcissistic partners can initially seem so appealing and why it can be so hard for those involved with them to break away, or choose someone different the next time around, or miss the warning signs early on. You will be introduced to *schema theory*, which explains how a child's unmet emotional needs lead to the development of *core beliefs* that underlie *life traps* (unhealthy life patterns), such as repeatedly engaging in relationships with narcissists. You will learn about the core beliefs that underlie the seven life traps most closely associated with women who are attracted to narcissistic partners, a combination of which may influence your dating choices. Examples will illustrate these various concepts. Sections called "Your Looking Glass" give you the opportunity to reflect on your childhood experiences, identify your core beliefs, and understand how they trapped you into repeating narcissistic relationships.

Why Are We Blind to the Warning Signs of Narcissistic Men?

To understand why we find narcissistic partners so appealing, we need to understand the negative psychological patterns we develop in childhood that tend to endure throughout our life unless we consciously change them.

Schema theory was developed and researched by prominent psychologist Jeffrey Young. In his original book on schema theory, *Reinventing Your Life*, he identified what he called *life traps*, self-destructive patterns of behavior which are formed as the result of negative experiences in childhood that happened to you.[2] We carry these life traps with us into adulthood, where we continue to reconstruct similar situations because they feel familiar to us, even if they are damaging. Women with specific life traps are doomed to repeat narcissistic relationships unless they become aware of their life traps and their underlying core beliefs (see below) and learn how to change them.

Core Beliefs

Core beliefs are the beliefs, which originated in childhood, that we that we hold about ourselves and the world around us. They color our perception of people and situations and influence how we feel and respond. For example, if I grow up in a family in which I am constantly criticized and my parents never tell me they love me, I will come to believe that I am unworthy of love. Believing I am unworthy of love becomes a core belief about myself, and I carry this belief from childhood into adulthood. It then affects all my relationships, especially intimate relationships, and influences my dating choices because I am vulnerable and desperate for affection, never having received it in childhood. As an adult, I may avoid intimate relationships altogether because I believe I am unworthy of love, or I may become attracted to the first man who shows me any attention. I will easily mistake attention for affection, which can be disastrous if he is not sincere. If he turns out to be a narcissist, the relationship is doomed. It will end, and I will interpret it as my fault since I believe I am unworthy of love, not knowing that it is actually my core belief and my desperation for attention that makes me vulnerable to my fated dating choices. So, I continually repeat this pattern with men who show me attention.

Core beliefs become the narrative themes in our life story. Our core beliefs underlie the way we think and act in the world and eventually become patterns of behavior because we view all our experiences through the prism of our core beliefs. These patterns of behavior are called *life traps* because they trap us in unhealthy ways of living and relating to the people, situations, and events of our lives.

Schema theory explains it this way: When a child's basic childhood needs—nurturance, empathy, love, security, and safety—are met, it creates a stable environment for the child, which supports the development of self-esteem, individuation, responsibility, self-expression, and self-control. This child believes she is lovable and deserves to be loved. She experiences self-acceptance, is unafraid to express her opinions, and feels free to explore and become whatever she chooses. On the other hand, another child whose most basic childhood needs go unmet may develop self-destructive patterns of behaving and interpreting life's events and situations. This child believes she is unlovable, flawed, or defective. She will continually pick partners who fit with her core beliefs about herself. So, we come to hold certain core beliefs about ourselves as a result of our childhood and adolescent experiences, and these beliefs trap us into repeating unhealthy relationships.

How Your Identity Is Shaped by Your Core Beliefs

Our core beliefs make up a significant part of the foundation of our identity and remain strong and stable throughout our lives. If those core beliefs are healthy ones (for example, I am worthy of love), they play a good and important role in our lives. If, however, our core beliefs are unhealthy (for example, I am *not* worthy of love), we need to identify and recognize them for what they are—unhealthy core beliefs—and consciously work to change them. Unhealthy core beliefs might sound something like "No one will be there for me," "Everyone lets me down," "There is no one I can count on," and so on.

For example, if I have the abandonment life trap, my core belief may be that everyone always leaves me. (For more on specific life traps, see "Life Traps and Core Beliefs" below.) So when I am in a relationship, I might be controlling or jealous because I am threatened by my belief that my partner is going to leave me for someone else. Or I might push my partner away so that I end the relationship on my terms before he can leave me. Core beliefs are the deeply rooted conclusions we hold about the world and ourselves.

Life Traps and Core Beliefs

Drawing on Young's work on schema theory, I identified seven life traps that are most clearly associated with women who are attracted to narcissistic men. Though there are other life traps, throughout this book we will focus on the seven listed below because they play such a big role in the lives of women attracted to narcissistic men.

Abandonment Life Trap: *You primarily feel rejection.*

Core belief: *People always leave you.*

Mistrust/Abuse Life Trap: *You feel hurt.*

Core belief: *People hurt or manipulate you.*

Emotional Deprivation Life Trap: *You feel misunderstood.*

Core belief: *No one is there for you.*

Defectiveness/Shame Life Trap: *You feel inadequate, unlovable, and unworthy.*

Core belief: *You are not good enough to love.*

Subjugation Life Trap: *You suppress your wants and needs in order to please someone else.*

Core belief: *If you don't meet someone else's needs, that person won't care about you. You do not have a choice.*

Self-Sacrifice Life Trap: *You feel responsible for others and feel guilty when you don't take care of others, but you also feel resentment at taking care of others.*

Core belief: *You need to help or fix others, and it is your choice to do so.*

Unrelenting Standards Life Trap: *You feel the need to strive to be the best in everything, to be or have things be perfect, or to follow self-imposed rigid rules.*

Core belief: *Whatever you do, it will never be good enough.*

As you look at the description of each of these seven life traps and their associated core beliefs, you may be saying to yourself, *Wow, that's me. I never realized how much I think this way.* And that is the point. Our life traps and core beliefs create ways of thinking and behaving that are so automatic that we take them for granted and never stop to realize how they direct our choices in men.

How Your Life Traps Have Influenced Your Dating Choices

According to schema theory, we are drawn to events, situations, and types of people who trigger our particular life traps because they feel familiar to us. So, for example, if your narcissistic parent was unable to unconditionally approve of you or failed to tune in to your emotional needs, you might seek a narcissistic partner who relates to you in a similar way (for example, makes you feel as if you are not valuable or that you are never good enough). It feels familiar somehow, like home. You may find that you try harder to meet your partner's expectations and demands to compensate for your core beliefs. The kicker is, you don't even know you are doing this. It just comes naturally.

Think back to Jessica's story. What attracted her to these men? What unmet childhood needs might she have had? What core beliefs do you think trapped her in repeating the same behaviors with the same type of partner?

Your Looking Glass

Before we go on, take a moment to reflect on what you've read so far and your own experiences from childhood. Notice how you feel emotionally and physically. What thoughts are going through your head *right now*? Write them in your journal. For example, you might be feeling sad, confused, uncomfortable, unsettled, anxious, or a bit nauseous. You may have thoughts like *I never feel good enough* or *I always assume men will leave me.* There are no right or wrong answers.

Let's return to Jessica's story now and discover what led to her attraction to narcissists. It was a spell cast when she was a child growing up in a dysfunctional family.

Parent-Child Relationships: How Life Traps and Core Beliefs Begin

Most parents mean well. It is not their intent to cause their child to have issues in life. I tell the women I work with that unless there is abuse, I don't like to blame parents. We discuss parents as a way to explain certain things many of us have come to believe about ourselves. Many parents are unaware they are causing problems in their child because they are blind to their own issues. Such was the case with Jessica. When she was growing up, her mother's needs and desires ruled the family. It was clear to Jessica at a very young age that her feelings did not really matter to her mother. The only time her mother seemed to approve of or pay attention to her was when she was catering to her mother's needs or fulfilling one of her mother's goals.

Jessica's mother never told her she was proud of her. In fact, as an adult, Jessica was surprised to learn from a good friend that Jessica's mother had always loved to brag to her friends about her daughter's accomplishments. Why couldn't her mother tell her instead of others? Jessica did try to please her mother, and on those rare occasions when Jessica went against her wishes, her mother would withhold love by conveying that she was terribly disappointed in her. For Jessica as a young girl, this was devastating and prompted a fear of losing her mother's love.

As for Jessica's father, he could not stand up to his wife. Jessica learned not to argue with her mother because her mother had all the power, and even her father could not protect her. So Jessica coped by keeping her true feelings to herself and acquiescing to her mother—and later to others.

As Jessica became a young adult, her mother began to live vicariously through her, prodding her to live the life she wished she had. Jessica should pursue a prestigious career, secure a prominent place in society, and marry a wealthy man. Jessica followed her mother's wishes as best she could but could not seem to check off that last box that would have made her mother so happy: marry a rich guy. It wasn't enough for her mom that Jessica was on track to become a dedicated internist with a thriving practice affiliated with a world-renowned medical center. Nothing ever seemed to be enough to please her mom. Although poised and soft-spoken, Jessica was under tremendous stress as she attempted to take care of her parents financially as well as satisfy her mother emotionally. But Jessica ignored her needs and suppressed her anger, telling herself that her parents needed her, believing that family should take care of family and that it was her role to be their financial caretaker since she was working.

Jessica's Life Traps

Jessica was dealing with several key life traps from her childhood: subjugation, self-sacrifice, and unrelenting standards, which resulted in certain behaviors, such as putting other people's needs first, neglecting herself, and suffering in silence. These life traps were founded upon essential core beliefs, such as "If I don't meet others' needs, they won't care for me," "I need to help or fix others," and "I need to do it better." Jessica learned to put other people's needs first, subjugating her own. Because her mother's needs always came first, falling into the trap of putting a narcissistic man's needs first felt natural. And since narcissistic men are utterly self-absorbed and require a woman to think only of their needs, they appeared to be the perfect fit for Jessica.

Jessica was attracted to wealthy men because of her need for her mother's approval. She was conditioned to seek wealthy men because anything less would not be good enough. Since she never felt whatever she did was good enough for her mother (unrelenting standards life trap), she became a workaholic. Jessica also perceived that the extra income would help pay for her parents' needs, which she was well accustomed to attending to because of her self-sacrifice life trap. Jessica was blinded not only by a prospective partner's money but also by his initial approval of her (approval she never received as a child), as well as by his Prince Charming demeanor (promising that her unmet childhood needs would finally be fulfilled). But by the time the "prince" revealed himself to be a narcissist, Jessica was already trapped. She put up with the horrible remarks and behaviors because she had already experienced the life trap of whatever she did, it was not good enough and held that core belief about herself. And she had learned from her mother that any direct challenge or resistance would result in the withholding of love. That feeling, much as she hated it, was familiar to her. Jessica was used to subjugating her needs to the needs of those closest to her (her mother, her lovers), so she changed her hair and clothes, tried to lose weight, and accepted a man telling her that her friends and family were not intellectual, trendy, or interesting enough.

Narcissistic men need their partner to look and act a certain way because their partners are merely "a reflection" and extension of them. It's all about *them*. If their partners are not "perfect," that is, do not live up to the narcissist's expectation, this stirs up their own feelings of inadequacy and insecurity. They may then use controlling, bullying, or intimidating behaviors to try to change their partners. This is why they cannot stick with a partner who challenges them or disagrees with them. So as long as Jessica went along with her narcissistic partners' precise demands, they kept her around. If she veered even slightly from their commands, they would not tolerate it.

Like so many other women, Jessica cannot help being attracted to narcissistic men because her core beliefs make her vulnerable to them. Once she becomes aware of those core beliefs and what she can do to change them, she will no longer be doomed to repeat the Todd/Ethan scenario.

The core belief that made up Jessica's self-sacrificing life trap is that if she doesn't fix or help others, she won't be loved or cared for. So Jessica felt responsible for her parents' happiness and financial stability. Her core belief formed a thick wall blocking her from the truth about her partners. But as she becomes aware of her core belief, she will begin to know the truth about herself and the partners she chooses. This knowledge will guide her toward healthier relationships.

Although Jessica repeated narcissistic relationships, Tess's story, which you'll read shortly, illustrates how you can overcome this fate through understanding your core beliefs and changing your life. Tess is a woman who overcame her unhealthy core beliefs, broke free from her self-destructive life traps, became her own "fairy godmother," and found her "happily-ever-after." (Being your own fairy godmother means giving yourself whatever you missed out on in childhood, including love and nurturing. (For more on being your own fairy godmother, see chapter 7.) In essence, when you become your own fairy godmother, you create your own "happily-ever-after"—and greatly increase the likelihood that you will end up in a relationship with a *healthy* Prince Charming. You really can create the life you always wanted.

Tess's Story

Tess was an only child to parents who were locked in an unhappy marriage. They were disengaged from each other and from Tess. They did not understand her or have empathy for her emotional needs, shaming her when she did find the courage to express them. Tess was left alone much of the time, and there was little interaction or enrichment at home. Being the sole breadwinner and an alcoholic, her father "retired" before he was fifty and put the family into a perpetual state of economic crisis. Tess's mother was a homemaker who found solace in religion and kept herself busy with religious activities, always going to meetings. Being in constant financial stress, Tess never experienced a family vacation, nor was she able to participate in her eighth-grade school trip to Washington, DC. Her parents denied her anything that young people might want in order to fit in with their peers—a certain color or style of notebook or backpack— and they mocked her for wanting these things. Being out of step with her peers, Tess felt ashamed and alone. As painful as this was, she never learned how to stand up for herself or get the help she needed. She developed the core beliefs that she was unlovable and unworthy of attention, that she had nothing to offer, and that no one would be there for her (based on her emotional deprivation and defectiveness/shame life traps).

At fifteen, Tess met a boy named Paul, whom she really liked. She finally got up the courage to invite Paul home, but her father was in the living room drunk, yelling and carrying on. Tess was so humiliated that she never faced Paul or dated again in high school, missing out on homecomings and prom. At sixteen, she tried to kill herself.

Fast-forward to Tess at age forty-four. Because Tess had experienced emotional deprivation as a child—growing up with parents who did not understand her emotional needs—she grew up feeling ashamed of herself. As an adult, she overcompensated for her feelings of shame by pursuing higher education, working in a challenging and satisfying career as a designer at a prestigious interior design firm, enriching her life with the arts, music, and theater, and creating a home that was filled with things that she loved. Now she had everything that she had been denied in childhood.

In addition to being an educated, interesting woman who had lived abroad for an extended period of time, Tess was also an excellent cook, a wine aficionado, and a foodie who often entertained. Despite all this, she continued to feel she did not fit in with others, was uninteresting, and had nothing to offer—especially to a man—and she was certain she would end up alone.

More than anything, she wanted to be married and have a family, but she kept being attracted to men who spent money on her and had status rather than men who valued love and commitment. She chose self-absorbed, emotionally cold and distant men who did not value her or validate her feelings. She never shared herself deeply with others because of her deep sense of shame, thus depriving herself of meaningful emotional connections with others. She kept up a public persona of happiness but drank alone at home to drown her painful feelings and loneliness.

When Tess came to me, she had a history of repeated failed relationships and had been dating an abusive man for nearly a year. Although highly educated, he was not successful and had had numerous business failures. And sometimes he was mean to her dog. In short, he was a real loser. In spite of these qualities, she had convinced herself that he would marry her and they would start a family, even though he said he was not sure he wanted one. Her desire for love and family overrode the red flags that were so obviously waving in front of her face. Eventually, she broke up with him, but then he suffered another business crisis, and she went back to him because she felt sorry for him. He seemed very appreciative but returned to being a jerk as soon as the crisis passed. Tess could deny the truth no longer and returned to therapy to figure herself out, once and for all.

Once we worked together to help her identify her core beliefs and life traps, she was able to move forward. She ended that dysfunctional relationship and was ready to take some risks of opening up to her girlfriends, asking people for what she wanted, and dating a new type of man.

A few months later, she reported that Paul, her first love from high school, had contacted her through social media. His return brought up painful memories of high school—not fitting in, the embarrassing incident with her drunken father—and she immediately declined his request to connect. When she told me she declined his request, I encouraged her to reconsider and accept his friend request, as did her girlfriends. The following session, she reported that she had accepted his request and that they had a first date planned. A true act of courage! He wasn't as polished and flashy as the men she usually dated—the men who never showed her respect or love. Paul was, however, college educated and worked in a family business. Also, he was close to his family and excited to share Tess with them. He loved her dog, and her dog was crazy about him.

Tess continued to date him, opening to his warmth and love yet going slowly and paying attention to her core beliefs. Tess did not fall head over heels as she had in the past. Now she is with a man who loves her and provides her with the large extended family she always wanted, and they are discussing starting a family of their own. She is happy for the first time. Today she is not holding back, feels more socially included, and is experiencing a steady increase in her self-esteem. Learning about her core beliefs helped shed light on her blind spots so that she could finally accept that she was good enough and that she was lovable. Though it took a while for these to become new core beliefs, Tess's work in therapy and her relationship with Paul helped her break free of her life traps and destructive core beliefs and eventually embrace healthier core beliefs.

How to Identify Your Core Beliefs

To understand why we are attracted to narcissistic men, we need to first look at ourselves through a process of self-reflection. Like the mirrors in fairy tales that tell you the truth about yourself and your life, self-reflection is a necessary skill that will help you to recognize your core beliefs and illuminate what traps you into repeating unhealthy relationships with narcissistic partners. In exercise 1 below, look at the list of statements about your thoughts, feelings, and behaviors while you're in your relationship(s). Your responses will help to clarify your core beliefs and how they contribute to your willingness to continue in that relationship. In the following chapters, you will continue to learn how your core beliefs originated and how they may have hindered your goal of a healthy relationship. Most important, you will learn ways you can change them.

Exercise 1: *Your Core Beliefs*

Which of the following apply to you currently or in your past relationships? You can write these down in your journal (or use the downloadable form for this exercise that's available at http://www .newharbinger.com/33674). You can also put the name or the first initial of any of your past partners next to them. For example, "I'm terrified of losing him." John, Dean. Or, J and D.

1. I'm terrified of losing him.

2. If he left, I would not be able to take care of myself.

3. Something is wrong with me; I'm flawed.

4. I never feel as if I fit in anywhere.

5. I often feel empty.

6. I don't know who I am.

7. I worry about terrible things happening that I will not be able to control.

8. I feel inadequate; I have always felt inadequate.

9. If this relationship fails, it means I've failed.

10. I avoid thinking about the negative aspects of my life or relationship.

11. I give in rather than have an argument.

12. I feel selfish if I want to do something my partner doesn't want to do.

13. I want people to think my life and relationship are wonderful.

14. If I am not perfect, everything will fall apart.

15. I try to do things so I won't be criticized.

16. I rarely meet my own expectations.

17. I find it difficult to relax.

18. I prefer to avoid confrontation.

19. I feel ashamed of myself.

20. I feel confused.

21. I've made excuses for him.

22. I feel I'm a burden.

23. *I walk on eggshells around him.*

24. *I believe he is a good person underneath.*

25. *No one knows him like I do.*

26. *I believe you make your bed and you lie in it.*

27. *I don't share my feelings about my partner or our relationship with others.*

28. *I often put his needs ahead of my own.*

As you considered which statements applied to you, did you notice any patterns? For example, did you notice that you put his needs ahead of your own, or you're afraid of failing and need to be perfect, or you sense that you're flawed and inadequate? Write the patterns you noticed in your journal. Looking at what you wrote, did it surprise you how many relationships you have had in which you had the same core beliefs or did the same behaviors?

Exercise 2: *Your Life Traps Associated with Narcissistic Partners*

Let's look again at the life traps associated with women who are attracted to narcissistic partners. (For the list of life traps, see "Life Traps and Core Beliefs" earlier in this chapter.) Look again at the list in exercise 1. Of those you selected, which life traps do you think correlate with them? Remember, it is common to have more than one life trap. Write your responses in your journal.

Great job! Did you have more than one life trap? If you did, remember having more than one is not unusual. Looking at your life traps, do you see a pattern? For example, if you feel defective and ashamed of yourself, you may have developed unrelenting standards and be driven to achieve to compensate for feelings of defectiveness and shame.

As you complete these exercises, I hope you have begun to gain awareness of how you behave in relationships, what attracts you to narcissistic men, and what motivates you to stay in destructive relationships. I also hope that you're more aware of the life traps that draw you into repeating narcissistic relationships. You will learn to further identify your life traps in chapter 3.

Putting It All Together

When any of our most basic childhood needs—nurturance, empathy, love, security, and safety—go unmet in childhood and adolescence, we develop negative core beliefs about ourselves and the world. These core beliefs may result in patterns of behavior, called life traps, that "trap" us into repeating unhealthy narcissistic relationships. As adults, we tend to be drawn to people who trigger our particular life traps because those traps feel familiar to us. This explains our attraction to narcissists (*Why do I keep repeating these types of relationships?*) and why we stay in these unhealthy relationships even when we know they are destructive (*Why I can't I leave?*).

In chapter 2, you will learn what narcissism is and what its origins are as well as the difference between healthy self-love and unhealthy narcissism. We will begin with the story of Narcissus.

The Frog: Understanding Narcissism and Narcissists

The word *narcissism* originates from the Greek myth of Narcissus, a handsome young hunter known for his beauty. According to the most common version of the myth, one day while in the woods, Narcissus stops to take a drink of cool water from a completely still, silver pond. When he kneels down at the edge, he sees his own reflection and falls in love with it. He tells the image, "I love you." Unable to pull himself away from the beauty of his own image, he disregards eating or drinking. Pining away for the image he has fallen in love with, he dies, eventually turning into the beautiful flower known as narcissus.

Well, the myth of Narcissus does not end with our self-enamored hunter. There is a beautiful nymph, Echo, who also finds herself attracted to the handsome but self-absorbed hunter—prior to his demise, of course! Is she doomed as well?

Echo: The Nymph Who Loved the Narcissist

Echo, a beautiful woodland nymph, had been punished by a god who took away her voice and only let her repeat what others were saying. Then, one day in the woods, she sees handsome Narcissus and is immediately smitten with his beauty. She follows him in the hope that he will say something kind and loving that she can then repeat back to him. So when she hears him say to his reflection, "I love you," she dreams that he will love *her* when he hears her repeat the words. She repeats, "I love you," but to her disappointment, Narcissus is so absorbed with his own reflection that he cannot hear her—or even see her. Echo is devastated. Try as she might, she has no effect on the object of her affection, and Narcissus never loves her. Echo withers away, waiting for his response, and eventually dies of unrequited love.

The story of Narcissus and Echo reflects the dynamic of today's narcissistic relationship. Narcissus is too self-absorbed to notice someone trying to love him; Echo keeps trying to be heard, only to be shut out. In another version of the story, Narcissus has so much pride that he is disgusted when Echo tries to love him. In that version, he hears Echo but shouts at her to be silent, just as in a modern-day relationship with a narcissist a woman will often provoke her partner's wrath when she says or does something he disagrees with. As in this mythological story, a person who has narcissistic self-love becomes destructive to himself and to others who try to love him.

Essential Elements

This chapter is about narcissism, the narcissist, and the woman who loves him. You will learn about the continuum of narcissism from the normal narcissistic needs we all have, such as feeling valued and loved, to the pathological form that makes up narcissistic personality disorder (NPD). This includes an excessive need for admiration, a lack of empathy, and the inability to see things from another person's perspective. You'll also learn how someone develops narcissistic personality disorder, why he very rarely changes, why you can't change him, and common threads among all narcissists. By looking at different patterns of behavior, you will learn how to recognize narcissistic traits in your partner.

Popular Definition of Narcissism

The popular definition of narcissism reflects the myth of Narcissus and refers to a person who is so absorbed with his own "self-love" that he cares little or nothing about anyone or anything else. This person, who can be male or female, has no authentic regard for the feelings of others and cannot see things from another's point of view. This can be confusing, though, because sometimes, especially in the beginning, he can act like he cares. Since he also lacks a strong sense of self, he needs constant admiration and validation from others. He is unable to accept faults in himself and therefore is intolerant of the faults in others. He is demanding, controlling, and difficult in relationships. Unable to accept blame or take responsibility for his mistakes, his needs in a relationship always come first. Today the word *narcissist* has become synonymous with a megalomaniac or egomaniac, someone who is dictatorial and arrogant. In reality, this only describes a narrow version of a narcissist. In the next section, we'll look at the different types of narcissists.

What Does a Narcissist Look Like?

Narcissists come in all shapes and sizes. This is why it can be so difficult for women to initially identify yet another narcissistic relationship. We all can pick up on the men with the obvious, obnoxious narcissistic traits—the grandiose, imperious, or pompous guys—and most women are not attracted to that boorish type of person or presentation. But if you define a narcissist by only those characteristics, you will be fooled and unprepared for the man who is just as authentically narcissistic but who has a far more subtle style.

In this quieter style, the narcissist you are attracted to appears thoughtful, caring, loving, and kind—in the beginning. You immediately feel comfortable around him, as if you've always known him. You find him easy to talk with, and you feel you can be yourself around him. You feel as if he "gets you" as no one ever has before. He's the one you've been waiting for. He is absolutely everything you ever wanted a man to be. The way he makes you feel is supremely seductive and intoxicating. Before you know it, you are deeply into him and the relationship.

A brief aside: As you read through this book, you may notice that the themes of beauty and wealth come up again and again. By no means do I encourage women to place an inordinate amount of attention on these qualities as they are growing and developing their sense of self. Our society does that for us enough. But I do want to point out that narcissistic men often seek out external, superficial indicators of a woman's worth, such as physical beauty that is deemed socially acceptable, fashionable dress, wealth, or personal and professional success. And some women who are susceptible to narcissistic men also try to compensate for their own lack of self-worth by overemphasizing physical attractiveness and wealth.

Narcissistic men look outside of themselves for validation and self-worth in such things as their employment status, achievements, or trophy wife. In other words, they are more interested in a woman's degree of socially recognized attractiveness or accomplishments than in her authentic self, because these things are a reflection of the narcissist's "success" in having "attained" a woman of stature. Other narcissists may look for a woman who admires them and makes them feel special, whereas still others may be attracted to women they believe they can control. These women often have low self-esteem and don't value themselves. Such women, because of their particular life traps, may be attracted to men who take control or are successful as a way to compensate for their own perceived shortcomings.

In time, the narcissist's true colors emerge, but you are too involved in your fairy-tale romance, too in love with the man you *want* him to be rather than the man he really is to see the red flags. Kate Winslet's character sums it up perfectly in the movie *The Holiday* when she answers her male friend's question, "Why am I attracted to a person I know isn't good?" Reflecting on her own unrequited love, she tells him, "Because you're hoping you're wrong, and everytime she does something that tells you she's no good, you ignore it, and every time she comes through and surprises you, she wins you over, and you lose that argument with yourself that she's not for you."[3] This quote says it all. We want to believe. We pin our beliefs on hope that we're wrong, that he'll return to the man we knew at the beginning. More times than I can count, I have heard women say these exact words to me: "He wasn't like that in the beginning." And the beginning was anywhere from months to thirty-one years ago.

People with a personality disorder have unhealthy ways of thinking and behaving that are rigid and pervasive throughout every aspect of their lives. They do not recognize that they have a problem and rarely seek therapy. So, what are the chances you'll encounter someone with a personality disorder, such as narcissistic personality disorder (NPD)? Here are the statistics we have today (as outlined in the *Diagnostic and Statistical*

Manual of Mental Disorders, 5th edition). In the United States, the rate of personality disorders is actually quite high, between 9 and 10 percent, on average. That means one in every ten individuals meets the criteria for a personality disorder. The current rate of NPD in this country is 1 percent of the general population, with 50 to 75 percent of narcissists being male. So although the chances of you finding and being in a relationship with a man with full-blown NPD may be well under 1 percent, the fact that you're reading this right now suggests that you may feel you seek these men out, or else they're drawn to you—and more than once. Let me tell you about Eva, a young professional woman I worked with who thought she had met a prince. She only paid attention to his stats—what he did for a living, how much money he made, what he looked like, what kind of car he drove, and so on—and not his values. She soon found out he was not her Prince Charming after all. Instead, he was a frog.

A Recipe for Disaster: Seeing Only What You Want

Eva was engaged in a longtime relationship that serves as one of many classic—and cautionary—tales. Michael first caught Eva's eye in a restaurant where she was dining with a girlfriend. She noticed how self-assured he seemed as he ordered the meal and the wine. He and his date seemed to be having a wonderful time. Later, when he caught Eva coming out of the ladies' room and asked her for her phone number, Eva was caught off guard but flattered. The fact that he was already on a date didn't even register. It should have.

Once they began dating, she was quickly pulled into his world. She did not object, happy to be with such a cultured man. Although Michael spoke French, knew wine, and loved jazz, he never flaunted his knowledge. He was polite, soft-spoken, and self-possessed, and he had definite ways of doing things. For example, after work, he'd have a glass of wine, listen to music, and read the paper or a journal. If she tried to start a conversation about her day, he would look at her, give a faint smile, and return to his reading. She felt she was intruding on his private sanctum if she spoke. She desperately wanted him to like her and to see her as sophisticated, so she began reading, too.

A month after they met, he told her he wanted to introduce her to his friends. She felt very special. He arranged a small, elegant soiree for sixteen people. Eva was a little intimidated, as his friends were impressive. She did think it odd that he didn't ask her to invite any of her friends, but she let that go. After all, it was *his* party, not hers.

Once on a ski vacation he looked at her as they were relaxing at the end of the day and shook his head admiringly, saying he had never thought he could be with a woman who looked like her. This made her feel so attractive and desirable that, when he began to get moody over trivial things, she ignored it, reassuring herself that everyone gets moody from time to time. But on her birthday, when she dared to wonder why he had not bought her a gift, he "snapped" and came right up to her, his face contorted, and screamed, "HAPPY BIRTHDAY!!!" She froze, and then started to cry. He looked at her in disgust, became cold and detached, and left the room. He did not try to comfort her. Where did the composed gentleman go? This happened one year almost to the day they started dating.

Unfortunately, scenarios like Eva's are not uncommon for the woman who is attracted to the narcissist. The trap of only paying attention to what we want or how we want things to be will come back to bite us every time because narcissists are masters at being what we want at the beginning of the relationship. However, even narcissists who appear in the subtler forms eventually show their true colors. That is why you need to understand the full range of narcissism, including the full-blown narcissistic personality disorder (NPD), so you do not unwittingly repeat another unsuccessful relationship.

Clinical Definition of Narcissistic Personality Disorder (NPD)

It is helpful to know the clinical definition of narcissistic personality disorder that professionals use. Many women I have worked with have said they were relieved to learn about narcissism and how narcissists look, relieved that there is a name for what they had been dealing with as well as a vocabulary with which to talk about it. Although the behaviors that mental health professionals use to diagnose someone with NPD are similar to the popular definition, it's when those behaviors become rigid and mis-directed that they can become seriously problematic. As you read the fol-lowing behaviors for NPD, remember that these behaviors have intensified and become seriously problematic. In its *Diagnostic and Statistical Manual of Mental Disorders,* 5th edition, the American Psychiatric Association says that those with NPD try to maintain their self-esteem through atten-tion and approval seeking and either obvious or subtle grandiosity. To have full-blown NPD, someone must have moderate to strong difficulty in two or more of the following areas of personality "functioning"—that is, the thoughts and behaviors affecting the way a person interacts with people and situations.

1. *Identity*: Narcissists continually look to others to see how they are doing and to maintain their self-esteem. Their view of themselves is often exaggerated, whether they see themselves as terrific or a victim, and so their mood fluctuates because it is tied to how they think or feel at any moment about themselves in relation to others. In other words, they do not have the ability to accurately see themselves and need to look to others for their sense of identity.

2. *Personal motivation*: Narcissists often choose goals only if those goals get them approval or kudos from others. In their need to be seen as special, they may set very high standards for themselves, such as getting to the top of a corporation, or they may have low standards if they believe they shouldn't have to comply with the rules. They might leave before 5:00 p.m. on workdays or routinely come in late.

3. *Empathy*: Narcissists have great difficulty or lack the ability alto-gether to recognize or identify with the feelings and needs of others. They can be excessively attuned to the reactions of others, but only if they believe it will be important or beneficial to them. They over- or underestimate their own effect on others. For example, they might assume others are in awe of what they just said or did, or they may not realize they just said something cruel

and hurtful to someone, thinking instead that it was not a big deal. Often, they simply don't understand why that person is getting so upset. They cannot see things from someone else's view or feel what that person feels, and therefore they do not understand the impact they have on another, particularly when it is negative. The other person's feelings simply do not matter, unless they serve the interest of the narcissist.

4. *Intimacy*: Narcissists' relationships are largely superficial and exist to maintain the balance of self-esteem. Relationships are hampered further because narcissists have little genuine interest in their partners' experiences and are more interested in what they can gain from the relationship.

Other areas that must be considered are the personality traits of grandiosity and attention seeking. Both of these must be present for a diagnosis of NPD.

1. *Grandiosity*: Narcissists feel entitled to do and say whatever they please, either obviously or on the sly. They are the center of their universe. They strongly believe they are superior to others, and because of this belief they treat others in a condescending manner.

2. *Attention seeking*: Narcissists need to be the center of attention at all times. They need to be admired and adored and seek out those who will put them on the pedestal they rightfully believe they own. Their need for attention and admiration is never ending, and so they constantly seek out "new" people and situations to feed this need.[4]

To make things more complicated, Wendy Behary, internationally respected expert on narcissism and best-selling author, describes in her book *Disarming the Narcissist* how narcissists wear different "masks," the most common of which are the bully, the show-off, the addictive self-soother, and the entitled one. They do this as a strategy to escape uncomfortable feelings. These narcissists, she says, can shift from one mask to another, depending on what's called for in the situation facing them.[5]

It's important to understand that a diagnosis of NPD can only be made by a trained mental health clinician. That doesn't mean you can't recognize the pathological behaviors in your partner, but only a clinician can make an actual diagnosis. If one of the women I work with describes her partner to me, but I haven't actually met him, the most I can say is that he *sounds as if he fits* the criteria for NPD. Unless your partner has actually been diagnosed by a clinician, the most responsible thing you can say is that he has most or all the traits of someone with NPD. Although many people may have narcissistic traits, simply having them does not indicate a full-blown narcissistic personality disorder. Nonetheless, depending on the traits and to what degree they're expressed, a relationship with that person can be difficult, unsuccessful at best and destructive at worst. And since it is rare for a narcissist to change, and rare, too, for such a relationship to ever become healthy, it may be best to let it go.

Your Looking Glass

How did that last statement—"it may be best to let [your relationship] go"—make you feel? Take a moment to record your feelings and thoughts in your journal.

***

Here, for example, is what Eva wrote:

Let him go? I feel scared and hopeless. But why? I need to recognize a narcissist sooner, and as much as I may want to believe the relationship will work out, I will save myself a lot of grief if I end it earlier. That doesn't mean I'll just book out of there at the first sign I think points to a narcissist, but I will pay attention, and if I see a pattern or I "feel" a pattern, I'll seriously think about leaving. And I need to pay attention to how I feel, think, and behave when I am with him. What is happening inside of me is important.

Another way to help you understand narcissism and narcissistic personality disorder is to view one's narcissistic needs on a continuum from healthy self-love to unhealthy narcissism. Yes, there is such a thing as healthy self-love, and it is not the same as being narcissistic. Oftentimes when I describe healthy self-love to a woman, she asks if that means she is being narcissistic, because she feels as if she is being selfish. The following section will explain the differences between healthy self-love and unhealthy narcissism.

Healthy Self-Love vs. Unhealthy Narcissism

Healthy self-love means loving and accepting yourself. When you can love and accept yourself, you are able to love another. If you haven't learned to love yourself, you are doomed to be attracted to and, in turn, to attract partners who can't give you love. When your partner can't love you, it feeds into your core beliefs—for example, that you are defective and unworthy of love. You will forever be in a vicious cycle of attracting partners who aren't capable of loving you because you believe you are unlovable or unworthy of love.

Healthy self-love also allows us to accept our faults as well as our strengths and to balance our needs with those of others. It means having a strong sense of self. This enables us to have give-and-take in our relationships, balance our needs with the needs of others, and understand ourselves. *Healthy self-love is different than having narcissistic personality disorder in that individuals with this disorder cannot feel empathy or see things from someone else's perspective.*

Payson's Healthy Self Continuum

It can be somewhat challenging to discern the differences between healthy self-love and NPD. Psychotherapist Eleanor Payson, who writes about healthy and unhealthy degrees of narcissistic need in her book *The Wizard of Oz and Other Narcissists*, offers a continuum from narcissistic *healthy self* to narcissistic *neurotic self* (some problems) to *full character disorder* (or narcissistic personality disorder). This is a quick way to view the differences between healthy narcissism (healthy self-love) and NPD.[6]

Healthy Self

- strong sense of self
- capacity to self-reflect, acknowledge problems, and take responsibility
- flexible defenses
- full capacity to empathize with others
- narcissistic needs in balance with awareness of others and their needs
- conscience fully developed
- self-esteem sturdy and resilient to the ups and downs of life

Neurotic Self

- overall intact sense of self
- ability to self-reflect, experience the pain of these problems, and have motivation for change
- defenses at times rigid
- significant capacity to empathize with others
- narcissistic issues connected to specific emotional problems
- low self-esteem issues common; becomes fragile when encountering difficulties connected to emotional wounds
- conscience developed with areas of distortion

Full Character Disorder (narcissistic personality disorder)

- severely impaired sense of self
- little or no capacity to observe self and acknowledge problems
- defenses rigid and brittle
- little or only superficial ability to empathize with others
- narcissistic issues connected to primary means of experiencing self
- conscience not fully developed or only marginally developed
- self-esteem merged with grandiosity and combined with defenses of "splitting" off parts of the unwanted self

Here Payson describes the difference between someone who is character disordered (has NPD) and someone who is neurotic:

> The character-disordered person is so disturbed that he is unable
> to see that he has a problem, while the individual who struggles
> with a particular neurosis is overall healthier, but unable to recog-
> nize their strengths.... The individual with neurotic issues needs
> help to identify her strengths and capabilities so that she can
> move on and enjoy her life.... [T]he capacity for observing your-
> self and working on these characteristics is the critical distinction
> between having narcissistic traits and the full blown disorder.[7]

In other words, while you may have psychological difficulties, the fact
that you can recognize and be concerned about them is what makes you
healthy versus character disordered. Furthermore, Payson writes that the
ability to self-reflect is a strength, not a weakness. According to Payson,
"Individuals with character disorder lack the ability to recognize that they
have a problem."[8] The following anecdote is about a man named David.
See if you can determine where David is on the continuum.

Does This Man Seem Familiar?

David, thirty-five years old, had been married six years and had one
child, age four. He had an MBA and had worked at the same corporation
for seven years. David's wife, Hilary, was very bright. They met ten years
before, when he was in his MBA program and she was studying to be an
attorney. Although he liked being around her, at times he felt she was
brighter than he was and that made him feel uncomfortable. To compensate for this feeling, he devalued her by finding flaws in the way she dressed
and things she said. He loved to entertain, holding court with guests while
his wife played hostess. He often took this too far, cutting people off, not
listening when others were talking, and nervously awaiting his chance to
reclaim the spotlight. Sometimes he brought up embarrassing stories
about Hilary at parties. He covered these insults by telling her he was just
joking. When she complained, he told her she was too sensitive and
needed to lighten up.

After the guests left, Hilary was left to clean up. He was always too tired to help. But he would hug and kiss her and tell her she was a good sport as he went upstairs to bed. Hilary would rationalize his not helping by telling herself that she could do it faster and that he was hopeless with such tasks and didn't know where anything went in the kitchen. As she cleaned up after the party, she reminded herself that he loved her. After all, he'd told her how impressed their guests were with their house, and that he appreciated her for pulling off the party.

On weeknights, he'd come home exhausted and complain about how stupid or incompetent his boss and/or coworkers were, often boasting how he had saved a situation from disaster with his talents and gifts. It frustrated him that his boss didn't acknowledge these contributions, and he'd often grumble to his wife about quitting his job because of his boss and coworkers' lack of respect and appreciation. Even though there had been complaints about David's management style and that he'd even caused an important project to be delayed, which almost cost the company a client, David never took responsibility. Instead, he would get more defensive, blame others, and threaten to quit. Hilary learned never to go against him on anything because he would never accept blame. And the fights just weren't worth it.

David loved his son, whom he considered a mini-version of himself. David would come home and revel in his son's adoration of him as the boy squealed with delight at just about anything his father did. When the son tried to change the play to something he liked, David would quickly lose interest and try to redirect him to what he was interested in or declare playtime was done. Seeing the disappointment on her son's face, Hilary would swoop in and take over.

Hilary had quit her job as an attorney when they had their son. She had been on partner track and would have made partner by age thirty, but David convinced her it would be better for the family if she stayed home. This arrangement mostly benefited David, who wanted a clean house and dinner at the end of the day, something a full-time attorney would not be able to manage. He did not want any part of coming home to an empty house and having to start dinner or pitch in more with child care and household chores. A new baby also meant interrupted nights, and David felt he couldn't afford to be sleep deprived at his job, so he played the guilt card, saying things like the baby needed his mother more than his father at this early stage. And she was, after all, breastfeeding. He told her she could always go back to work later when their child was grown.

Hilary reluctantly gave up her career in the interest of being a good mother and supportive wife. The arrangement worked well enough at first, but soon David began to change, becoming very controlling with money and requiring Hilary to get his permission to buy anything and to justify everything she bought. The fights over money wore her out, so she often just gave in. He could never see her side of an argument. He also became more controlling in other areas of her life. He would get angry if the house was not in order or if their son acted up. He pouted if she was going out to do something for herself. He complained about her body after she had the baby. She began to feel less and less like herself.

David's constant criticisms further eroded her sense of self. She tried to be a better mother and wife to gain his approval and recover her self-esteem, but he always made her feel as if somehow she had not done enough. The accomplished, smart, self-confident attorney on partner track was now a vague memory. She still loved him and longed for how they were when they first met. He'd been so attentive and loving. Now they were rarely intimate.

Where do you think David falls on the continuum of healthy versus character disordered narcissism? It might be helpful to first identify some of his narcissistic traits from the *Diagnostic and Statistical Manual of Mental Disorders* (DSM-5),[9] along with examples. You can add more if you like.

Envious: Feels Hilary is brighter than he is, so he devalues her.

Need for admiration: Loves to entertain and hold court, be the center of attention.

Lacks empathy: Cuts others off and is unaware of his wife's and son's needs. Doesn't see or understand when he has hurt his wife's feelings, nor does he seem to care.

Self-serving: Asks Hilary to become a stay-at-home mom.

Grandiose: Believes he is saving the day at work.

Cannot accept he has a problem: Blames others such as his wife, boss, or coworkers.

Looking at these traits, where would you put him on the continuum? If you said the character-disorder end of the continuum, you would be correct.

After reading about David, you may be wondering how he became this way. How do narcissists become narcissists? There are specific reasons why narcissists become narcissists, and it has to do with their childhood experiences, just like your life traps.

Origins of Narcissism

Why do some people develop into full-blown narcissists while others do not? Are they somehow predisposed to it from birth? Is it hereditary? Environmental? Research has come up with explanations that will help you identify and recognize this condition so that you can protect yourself from unwitting alliances with men who suffer from it.

As I suggested in chapter 1, children develop negative ways of responding to their environment when their essential childhood needs—nurturance, empathy, love, security, and safety—are unmet. It is these unmet needs that underlie the development of narcissism in a child. Schema theory suggests several parenting models in which a child's basic needs are not met that can result in a child becoming narcissistic: the indulging parent, the overprotective parent, and the neglectful, detached, and/or abusive parent. These models can include one or both of the parents or caregivers. Let's take a look at each one of these parenting models in depth.

The Indulging Parent

This parent does not set effective limits or discipline the child; the child is allowed to break rules with few consequences. Because he is indulged, he never learns to tolerate frustration and therefore cannot manage his emotions when his expectations are not met. He will often resort to throwing tantrums to get his way.

As an adult, he continues to assume that all his expectations will be met, and as a partner, he may be demanding, controlling, and always feeling that he is entitled to anything and everything. He may be manipulative in order to get his way, and he may attack or devalue anyone or anything that frustrates him. Often he does not work well on a team because he has not learned the art and value of reciprocity. In relationships, a narcissist from this parenting model may be very controlling and demanding of his partner. He may own his own business because he cannot work under someone else or get along with coworkers. He may insist his partner and children live up to his unrealistic standards, but he can break his own rules any time he wants. For example, he may keep them on a tight budget but go out and buy some expensive toy just because he wants it. He may justify it as a birthday present for his wife, even though she did not want it. If she complains, he sulks, pouts, or gets mad at her.

The Overprotective Parent

This parent does everything for the child, trying to protect him from disappointment. Despite these seemingly good intentions, this parent does the child a great disservice because the child grows up feeling incompetent, the very opposite of what the parent hopes for the child. These children are fearful of living in the world or of making a mistake. They grow up expecting everything to be done for them and never have to face reality.

As a partner, the child of such parenting will expect you to take care of him, and when you don't, he'll become angry, put you down, or withhold love. In the realm of work, he may have never developed a good work ethic but will instead try to circumvent his responsibilities or take shortcuts. On the other hand, he may overcompensate for his fears of the world or of making a mistake by working even harder to avoid making those mistakes. But if he does make them, he will usually blame others. He may be a workaholic, not because he loves his career, but because he needs to know everything and wants never to get caught having made a mistake. Although married with children, he is driven to get up at 3:30 a.m. to drive to work. He works late into the evening, often coming home after 9:00 p.m. Despite ongoing objections from his wife, he continues with his agenda and dismisses her complaints. When his wife leaves him, citing the fact that he is never home and that she has met someone who treats her with love and respect, he feels as if he is the victim. After all, he worked those long hours for his wife and family. He is sincerely shocked at having lost them.

The Neglectful, Detached, and/or Abusive Parent

This type of parent does not provide love, safety, or nurturance to the child, or if he or she does, it is conditional, offered only when the child "delivers" something to the parent, such as good behavior, high grades in school, or some talent or ability. These parents, on a spectrum ranging from detached to neglectful to abusive, raise children who as adults feel love can only be obtained through manipulation. They have learned not to expect love. They may not trust others and may develop a sense of being in relationships for themselves. As a partner, a child brought up this way may easily become cold and detached and not allow himself to feel his own or anyone else's pain. He may become an over-achiever driven toward success, a workaholic, type-A perfectionist. He will continually feel unlovable and seek ways to feel better through addictive, self-soothing behaviors involving substances, gambling, or risk-taking adventures. He may be a stock market trader, a form of legalized gambling. His mood is contingent on his daily success as a trader. Or he may have a serious drinking and/or substance abuse problem, such as cocaine addiction. He expects his partner to be there for him all the time, regardless of his behavior.

Your Looking Glass

Let's check in: What feelings come up for you after reading this section? Can you think of someone you know who may have been raised with one of the parenting styles we just covered? How does knowing this change your perception of the men you've been with? Take some time now to reflect on these questions and write your responses in your journal.

***

Here's what Eva wrote:

> *It's helpful to understand how narcissists become narcissists. I had never thought about it before. I didn't understand how involved it was and how far back it began. It made me think about my last ex. His family was so dysfunctional. His mother was so detached and his father was an abusive alcoholic. There was no one in his corner. I guess that's why I could overlook so much of his bad behavior. I felt sorry for him. But no matter how much I tried, I couldn't change him or help him. Now I know why. I really couldn't—not because of some flaw within me but because it was beyond me. It will take him to change him, not me. It's not me. I am getting that now. No wonder I could never make it work.*

Common Threads in All Narcissists

Although narcissism develops through a variety of unmet childhood needs, it all boils down to a core of insecurity. When I work with women in my practice, I describe the two main features I see in narcissists: the insecure little boy and the seesaw phenomenon.

The Insecure Little Boy

Regardless of the type of narcissist he appears to be on the outside (grandiose or subtle), he is sure to be insecure on the inside as a result of his childhood experiences. This is often difficult for some people to understand, given the confidence many narcissists exude. But narcissists try to avoid painful feelings at all costs, and they have developed a thick defensive armor to fiercely protect that insecure little boy.

Many women involved in narcissistic relationships understand this about their partner, but unfortunately this very knowledge is what keeps them in the relationship, however destructive it may be for them. They have seen the insecure, scared little boy dwelling inside and hold on to that as a reflection of the man he is, ignoring the rest of his often unacceptable behavior. By soothing and protecting that little boy, they feel special and needed: only they can really understand him. They will often defend their partner's behaviors to others (and themselves), claiming they know him in a way that others do not. This is actually codependency, a dynamic we will examine more closely in chapter 3.

The Seesaw Phenomenon

Narcissists need to feel equal or superior to everyone and everything around them. Exquisitely sensitive due to their deep sense of insecurity and inadequacy, they continually assess where they stand in relation to everyone else. Think of the narcissist sitting on a seesaw, the kind we played on as kids with someone or something on the other end; the narcissist needs to keep that seesaw completely even or his end in the superior position. And he is so sensitive that the slightest perceived threat to this arrangement—however trivial and/or irrational it may be—triggers his defenses, causing him to attack or devalue. Mental health professionals refer to these perceived affronts to the narcissist as *narcissistic injury*, meaning the narcissist feels psychologically assaulted, and so to manage the pain or to get rid of it, he lashes out at whomever or whatever he feels hurt him. Of course, this all happens quickly and at an unconscious level. Let's look at a couple of examples of this behavior.

The narcissist is at a party. Someone brings up a topic he's unfamiliar with and teases him for not knowing about it, or someone else mentions a fantastic recent vacation to a place he has never been. Anything that causes the narcissist to feel less than the other will stir up his deep sense of insecurity and inadequacy, and because he cannot tolerate these painful feelings, he will immediately attack or devalue in order to feel that he's at least equal to the other. It's a zero-sum game: someone else's perceived strength or achievement inevitably means equivalent diminishment for him, and vice versa.

Here's another example. Sarah helps her husband in their real estate business. She's been particularly good at finding houses or apartments for them to *flip*, or renovate and sell at a higher cost, and clever at redecorating them so they'll flip faster. Whenever her husband comes to inspect a place she has finished remodeling and decorating, he can only comment on something that's off, like the empty bucket in the hallway that she fully intended to take with her upon leaving. He cannot compliment her on her hard work and lovely results. Seeing what a great job she's done sparks his insecurity, so he must devalue her efforts in order to feel better about himself. So when the narcissist's insecurities get triggered, and he lashes out overtly or covertly to even the playing field, this comes from his narcissistic injury, his feeling of being psychologically assaulted.

Exercise 3: *Identify Your Narcissistic Partners*

So now that we've discussed narcissism in more depth, does any of this sound familiar to you? Does your partner need to be the center of attention? Does he, for example, monopolize conversations or make everything about him? Does he pout or sulk when he doesn't get his way? Is it difficult or impossible for him to see things from another person's perspective? This exercise will help you determine if any or all of the partners you have been with are narcissists. It will also help you see if there is a pattern to the types of men you pick as partners.

You can complete the exercise in two ways: (1) Circle the number(s) of the question(s) that describes your partner(s), write those numbers in your journal, and then write the name(s) of the partner(s) after the applicable number, or (2) write everything in your journal—first the number(s) of the questions that describe your partner(s) and then the name(s) of your partner(s) to which that question applies. These questions are also available in a form that you can download by visiting http://www.newharbinger .com/33674, if it's easier to work with them that way.

His Behaviors with You

1. Was he exceedingly charming when you first met him? Did he sweep you off your feet?

2. When you were dating, did he respect your boundaries? For example, one woman's first date came in her house and opened her refrigerator looking for a late-night bite to eat without first asking her!

3. Did you find out disturbing truths or something shocking about him after you had been with him for a long while that he had kept secret from you? For example, he was married before, has a child with someone else, has a terrible credit history or gambling debt, or has been in prison?

4. Does he always criticize or put you down? For example, does he criticize small things like how you brush your teeth or answer the phone, how you dress, how you clean the house or raise the children? Does he criticize your job, family, or friends? Does he put you down for something you thought you did well (like when you reupholstered a chair)?

5. Does he keep promises and commitments to you?

6. Does he complain about being bored with you, with your family, or with situations or events? For example, does he say your family is not intelligent enough for him to spend time with, or an event you'd like to attend is too boring for him to waste his time at, so you end up canceling or going alone?

7. Are most things he does self-serving, but he insists he is doing them for you or the children or others? For example, does he spend money on something he wants, such as fishing equipment, but says it's because it'll be valuable for your son to learn how to fish? Or does he buy a big smart TV because the whole family will enjoy it, but he really monopolizes it to watch the sports programs he wants to watch?

8. Do you feel like he is a different person with others than he is with you? Do you think others would believe you if you told them what he was like at home? For example, a woman had a husband who was renowned in his field and prominent in their community. Everyone loved and respected him. He was kind and thoughtful to everyone—except to her at home. There he was controlling, horribly demeaning, and bullying.

9. Do you always find yourself having to defend yourself when you are trying to discuss something that he did wrong? For example, does he make the problem about you by bringing up how you did something wrong?

10. Does he contradict himself when you discuss things? Does it make you feel like you are crazy? For the record, you are not crazy if you find that you can never win an argument with him. Narcissists are experts at making you doubt your position on something—on anything.

His Behaviors in General

1. Can he accept responsibility for his mistakes, or does he blame others for them? If he is caught in a mistake or lie, does he play the victim?

2. Does he show remorse or guilt if he hurts you or someone else emotionally, physically, professionally, or financially?

3. Is he irresponsible with finances? For example:
   - Does he have a poor credit history?
   - Does he manage his money poorly?

- Does he pay bills late?
- Does he ignore the budget?
- Does he spend money as he likes without regard to consequences?

4. Does he throw an adult temper tantrum (for example, scream, yell, throw something, or threaten to leave) in an attempt to get his own way?

5. Does he have or has he ever had any addictions, like drugs, alcohol, or gambling?

6. Is he hotheaded? Does he overreact to situations (for example, by becoming quickly angry if someone cuts him off on the freeway, if there is a traffic delay, or if he is charged a finance fee for a late payment)? If so, does he have difficulty calming down afterward?

7. Does he bully or intimidate others to get his way, especially those he considers subordinate to him, like a bank teller or parking attendant?

8. Does he monopolize conversations? Does he need to be a know-it-all or to be the center of attention?

9. Does he lack a stable employment history?

10. Does he lack realistic long-term goals?

Any one of these questions describes someone who is likely narcissistic. Take another look at the "Clinical Definition of Narcissistic Personality Disorder" earlier in this chapter. Did your partner(s) fit the traits for narcissistic personality disorder? Remember, only a qualified mental health professional can diagnose a personality disorder. However, this exercise can help you identify narcissistic traits that your partner(s) may have as well as see if there is a pattern in the types of partners you pick. If many or all the partners you pick have narcissistic traits, you are repeating unhealthy narcissistic relationships. This book will help you stop repeating your pattern of unhealthy relationships.

Your Looking Glass

Let's check in. What are your thoughts and feelings about this exercise? Look at the questions you circled. Think about your partner(s), if you have had more than one narcissistic partner. Was there a common narcissistic behavior among them? For example, perhaps they all overreacted to situations, or they were all critical of you, or you could never discuss a problem without them verbally attacking you or making you doubt your position. Take a few moments to reflect and write your thoughts and feelings in your journal.

***

Eva wrote this:

Wow, I put a name next to over two-thirds of these questions! Many of the men I have been involved with had the same behaviors. I never took a tally like this before. I see how they were all narcissists. Although they did appear slightly different, they still had very similar traits. I thought they were all so charming in the beginning. We had chemistry, and we got together really quickly. I felt each of them really understood me—at least in the beginning.

Putting It All Together

We've covered lots of important ground in this chapter! You learned the definitions of narcissism and the criteria used by professionals to diagnose people with NPD. You also learned the difference between healthy and unhealthy self-love. You found out what the origins of narcissism are and what it looks like in childhood and in adulthood. You looked at the behaviors of your partners and answered questions about your relationships. In the next chapter, you will learn to identify experiences in your own childhood that have resulted in your particular core beliefs—those that prompt you to choose to be—and stay—in relationships with narcissists.

CHAPTER 3

Unmet Childhood Needs: Discovering Your Story

Do you ever fantasize that Prince Charming will swoop you up, and together you and the prince will live happily ever after? If you do—and who among us hasn't fantasized this way at some point in our lives—this fantasy makes you susceptible to being in a relationship with a narcissist. He makes you feel special because he chose you, similar to the fairy tale of Cinderella where Prince Charming chooses her out of all the girls in his kingdom.

Many of Cinderella's childhood needs, such as nurturance, empathy, love, security, and safety, were not met by her stepmother. Cinderella's story shows many of the kinds of childhood wounds experienced by the women I work with, and it may show the wounds you've experienced as well. Many children grow up in families where their parents may have meant well, but because of their own emotional problems and/or how they were raised, they actually harmed their children. As I've said before, I don't like to blame parents for the emotional problems their children have, unless there is abuse, because I believe parents, in most cases, do not intend to harm their children. But part of your healing process involves thinking back to when you were a child, and from that perspective—your perspective as a child—identifying the thoughts and feelings that led you to have certain core beliefs and life traps. It's the core beliefs and life traps that you still hold today that make you susceptible to the narcissist. Only in identifying and changing these core beliefs and life traps will you learn how to recognize a healthy partner in love.

Essential Elements

This chapter focuses on the childhood experiences of women who, as adults, are attracted to narcissistic partners. You will learn three key concepts that have a role in the development of your core beliefs and life traps, which in turn impact your dating choices and subsequent relationships: (1) shame and vulnerability, (2) coping through overcompensation, surrender, and avoidance, which correspond to the threat responses of fight, flight, and freeze, and (3) codependency behaviors. The underlying feelings of shame and vulnerability affect the way you cope and behave.

Shame and Vulnerability

Shame and vulnerability are very powerful feelings that develop when our childhood needs are not met, when we are told we are not good enough, when we are constantly criticized, when we don't have the things other children have, or when we don't have anyone in our corner. We come to believe we are whatever we've been told (either directly or indirectly)— that we are bad, inadequate, incompetent, or defective.

The Role of Shame

Shame is the painful emotion we experience when we believe we are inadequate or worthless. It is a very powerful feeling that traps us and stops us from sharing ourselves completely with another.

Shame is a destructive force in a young child's life. As a child, you came to believe that the "real you" had flaws the magnitude of which are beyond redemption and that you must never tell anyone what they are. To manage the painful feelings associated with your shame, you adopted certain *coping styles*, or ways of coping. For example, you may have tried to overcompensate by being the perfect child, getting good grades, or becoming a popular cheerleader. You may have surrendered to your shame by withdrawing and isolating yourself. Or you may have tried to avoid your shame by keeping it hidden. Regardless of how you tried to cope with your shame, it was always there, taking a toll on you. In fact, shame has been strongly associated with depression, eating disorders, addictions, bullying, and suicide.[10]

You weren't born feeling ashamed of yourself. No child is. Rather, you came to this belief as a result of childhood experiences that wounded you—experiences in which, tacitly or explicitly, through the words and/or behaviors of people who were supposed to love and care for you, you got the message that you were terribly flawed. For example, you may have been raised in a family in which you were constantly criticized, rejected, misunderstood, hurt, abused, or neglected, or where you had to suppress your wants and needs in order to receive love. Maybe you had a parent who was controlling or had high standards that you could never live up to, or maybe you were constantly compared to an older sibling or someone else's child, or maybe your parents didn't pay much attention to you. Any one of these experiences, or a combination of them, could result in deep shame about yourself and the core belief that you aren't good enough or worthy of love.

You then carried this shame into adulthood. I have witnessed how childhood shame negatively affects the lives of women in my practice who have ended up in narcissistic relationships. These women allow themselves to be mistreated, controlled, or criticized as they strive to be more perfect for their partner or to meet their partner's desires, needs, and expectations. They always put themselves last, never speaking up because they have come to believe they are unworthy of love and belonging—that is, being accepted and supported by others. But if they do speak up or put their own needs before those of their partners, they feel guilty.

Shame is not the same as guilt. *Guilt* is a feeling about a behavior you did, whereas shame is a belief about yourself because of the behavior you did. Guilt is "I did something bad," and shame is "I *am* something bad." Guilt is "I'm sorry I made a mistake," whereas shame is "I *am* the mistake."[11] When you believe that you are the mistake, you won't allow others to get close to you. Yes, you will feel safer by keeping what you're ashamed of a secret, but if you're trying to find a loving and caring partner to share your life with, you'll have great difficulty doing that as long as you keep a part of yourself hidden from your partner.

The Risk of Being Vulnerable

All children are inherently vulnerable because they are unable to care for themselves until they are older. They must rely on their parents or caregivers for protection and nurturance. Children who grow up in homes where they are loved, protected, and nurtured grow into adults with a secure sense of who they are, which includes self-acceptance and self-love, strong values, and being capable of loving another. They are able to take risks, to be open to others, and to be vulnerable because they feel secure within themselves.

But those unfortunate children who grow up without love, protection, or nurturance are more likely to lack a strong sense of self, resulting in lower self-confidence and self-esteem. Without a strong sense of self, they are vulnerable to exploitation and abuse by others. They have not learned how to protect themselves or how to discern danger in situations or people. They may have learned, however, that it's safer to be passive to avoid emotional or physical abuse. Because of their childhood experiences, they have not learned how to ask for what they need. And, because they were not valued as children, they don't value themselves, which leads to a feeling of shame about themselves.

If you experience shame, you face a dilemma: in order to be authentic, you have to trust another person and reveal that which you truly believe will cause you to lose that person's love. People with deep feelings of shame are not willing to be that vulnerable. It's simply too risky. For you as a child, this may have been a way to survive because it was too dangerous to express the real you. Being a child, it is almost certain you couldn't take that risk, so you lived with shame. Then you carried it into adulthood. And now that you're an adult, it negatively affects all your relationships.

But that way of coping, hiding a part of yourself as a way to protect yourself, no longer works. In order to be in a healthy relationship as an adult, you have to take the risk to be yourself, warts and all. It takes courage to be vulnerable, but it is absolutely worth the risk. You can see how shame and vulnerability go hand in hand. In order to free yourself from shame, you have to take that risk and be vulnerable by revealing your true self.

When finally as an adult you take the risk to be vulnerable and look at and expose your shame, you will find that the only person judging you is yourself. You're the one who continues to perpetuate your shame. You do this by holding on to your shame, which keeps you from healing your childhood wounds.

As you work through this book, I hope that you will learn to take the risk to be vulnerable. By breaking your silence, you lift the shade of shame and secrecy.[12] Shame and vulnerability researcher Brené Brown writes, "Owning our story can be hard but not nearly as difficult as spending our lives running from it. Embracing our vulnerabilities is risky but not nearly as dangerous as giving up on love and belonging and joy—the experiences that make us the most valuable. Only when we are brave enough to explore the darkness will we discover the infinite power of our light."[13] My hope is that you will be brave, explore your darkness, and discover your light. It is there, waiting for you to discover it.

Your Looking Glass

Before we go on, take a moment to reflect on what you've read so far about shame and vulnerability and your own experiences from childhood. Notice how you feel emotionally and physically. What thoughts are going through your head *right now*? Write them in your journal.

As children, we struggled to cope with our painful circumstances. The wounds we experienced resulted in core beliefs and life traps that weighed us down then, and continue to weigh us down now, with shame. Now let's look at how children cope with their difficult childhoods. You may have coped in one—or all—of these ways yourself.

How Children Cope: Overcompensation, Surrender, and Avoidance

Schema theory describes three coping styles children use to manage painful situations as overcompensation, avoidance, or surrender. Wendy Behary has linked these coping styles with children's reactions when they're afraid: (1) fight (overcompensation), (2) flight (avoidance), and (3) freeze (surrender).[14] Ironically, overcompensation (fight) often causes us to do the opposite of our life trap. For example, if your life trap is "defectiveness" (that is, deep inside you feel you are defective), as a child, you may have gone to great lengths to feel special in some way, which is the opposite of feeling defective. If you used avoidance (flight) as a way to cope, you would have avoided people and situations that made you feel defective. If you used surrender (freeze) to cope, you simply accepted your life trap and stayed passive yet unhappy. For example, you may have resigned yourself to being constantly criticized and stopped standing up for yourself. By doing this, you could avoid an argument in the short run, but, in the long run, you were unhappy because you were constantly criticized.

Although a child may use any one or all three ways of coping, usually one style predominates. Children who develop a life trap as a result of their childhood experiences will cope in a way that is appropriate for their temperament and personality: one may use avoidance for the defectiveness life trap, while another may use overcompensation. Each coping style may help the child cope at the time, but, in the end, these ways of coping don't change the life traps. Why? Because these coping styles are ineffective.

The coping styles we used in childhood follow us into adulthood. However, those styles that were helpful in childhood are not usually helpful in adulthood. In other words, using them won't help you to get your needs met. For example, if you used surrender as a child when there was a threat of conflict, you won't know how to manage conflict appropriately as an adult, and so you may give in to everyone. If you used avoidance as a child by overeating, you may find you still soothe yourself with food as an adult, but now you have a weight problem that perpetuates your low self-esteem; or worse, you have graduated to drinking alcohol to numb your emotional pain. What often happens is that the coping style that worked for you as a child later becomes a disservice to you, yet you are stuck with it until you learn new and healthier ways to cope. If you are attracted to narcissists as an adult, it is important for you to recognize and understand your childhood coping styles because they may very well be blocking you from getting what you truly need and deserve.

Your Looking Glass

Before we go on, take a moment to reflect on what you've read so far about these three coping styles—overcompensation, avoidance, and surrender—and your own experiences from childhood. Notice how you feel emotionally and physically. What thoughts are going through your head *right now*? Write them in your journal.

Another unhealthy behavior is codependency. Codependency needs to be recognized and understood on its own because it is such a self-destructive behavior and so common in women who choose narcissistic relationships. Let's take a closer look at codependency now.

Codependency

Most often when we think of codependence, we think of adults and substance abuse. The codependent adult tries to fix another person's substance abuse problem. This is a common but narrow definition of codependency. A broader definition of codependency, and the way I will use it here, is by best-selling author Melody Beattie, who has written about codependency for over thirty years. In her famous book *Codependent No More: How to Stop Controlling Others and Start Caring for Yourself*, she writes that "a *codependent person* is one who has let another person's behaviors affect him or her, and who is obsessed with controlling that person's behavior."[15] The obsession with trying to fix another person becomes an automatic habit—we do it without even realizing it.

Codependent behaviors, such as putting other people's needs ahead of our own or trying to control or fix people around us, originate in childhood as a way to protect ourselves and get our needs met. The problem is that we carry our codependent, self-protective childhood behaviors with us into adulthood, where they become destructive to us. Despite their destructiveness, we keep doing them because they are ingrained habits.

Many children try to protect themselves by focusing on the needs of others. For example, because of a fear of being abandoned, children may try to hold on to a depressed parent in any way possible so the parent won't leave. (This early fear of abandonment eventually develops into a life trap.) These children may try to cheer their parent up, giving up their own time and energy in an effort to make their parent happy. Other children may believe giving and helping others is a virtue, and so they give tirelessly of themselves to others. They believe they are being selfless and helpful even as they neglect their own wants and needs. (This eventually becomes the self-sacrifice life trap.) These codependent behaviors can be thought of as a form of the overcompensation coping style, because the children try to overcompensate for their fear of abandonment by trying to fix a parent, make a parent happy, or do any number of other behaviors that focus on the parent's needs rather than their own. Thus, children's codependent behaviors may be present in all seven life traps associated with women who are attracted to narcissistic partners.

Children who adopt these codependent behaviors and subsequent coping styles as a way to survive in childhood almost certainly end up being taken advantage of in adulthood. They are the perfect victims for the narcissist, who is only too happy to take advantage of someone willing to be devoted to him, someone who is focused on trying to meet all his needs. It is a distorted, symbiotic relationship in which the codependent woman feels driven to help the narcissistic man to get his needs met, but in the end the codependent woman never gets her *own* needs met. She is repeatedly attracted to people whom she perceives as needing her. Does any of this sound familiar?

What's the problem here? As hard as the codependent woman tries, the narcissistic man does not change. Or if he does, it is only for a short while, which only reinforces the codependent woman's resolve to continue trying. The heart of the problem actually lies in the codependent woman who sacrifices *all* her wants and needs in the service of the narcissistic man. (In fact, by doing this, a woman may get to the point where she no longer even knows what her wants and desires are.) These codependent behaviors that were adopted in childhood become habits that lead women deep into destructive narcissistic relationships that don't work. And we keep repeating them.

Your Looking Glass

Before we go on, take a moment to reflect on what you've read so far about codependency and your own experiences from childhood. Notice how you are feeling emotionally and physically. What thoughts are going through your head *right now*? Write them in your journal.

Putting It All Together

In this chapter, we focused on your childhood. Shame and vulnerability have a powerful impact on you not only as a child but also later as an adult. To manage your painful experiences as a child, you may have used overcompensation, surrender, and avoidance, which are ways of coping that correspond to the threat responses of fight, freeze, and flight. These ways of coping can be expressed in a variety of behaviors. You may have used one or more coping styles as a child, but you probably picked one as your dominant way of coping. You carry the coping styles that you used as a child into adulthood, where they may work against you and block you from getting your needs met. Another way of coping is codependency, which has a negative impact on you by causing you to neglect yourself in the service of others.

In later chapters, we will discuss adult codependency in more depth and talk about how to change it. But for now, let's turn to chapter 4. As you read the various childhood stories there, see if you can identify which children will end up with adult codependency issues, how shame impacted them, and which ways of coping they chose in order to survive.

A Closer Look at Life Traps

Your attraction to narcissistic partners started a long time ago, when your basic childhood needs of nurturance, empathy, love, security, and safety were not met. That early childhood wounding set you up to be the prey of a narcissist. While growing up, you came to hold certain negative beliefs about yourself. To counter these beliefs and manage painful childhood experiences, you adopted various coping styles and ways of behaving in the world, which eventually became life traps. Those life traps then allowed you to be attracted to narcissistic partners.

Essential Elements

In this chapter, we'll look at childhood examples that illustrate how unmet childhood needs result in negative core beliefs. These core beliefs underlie each of the seven life traps associated with women who are attracted to narcissistic partners. For each of the seven life traps, we'll hear the childhood stories of three different women. Their stories illustrate the various ways in which these life traps can be manifested depending upon life circumstances and the unique personality and temperament of the child.

Seven Life Traps and Core Beliefs Refresher

Before we continue, let's take a moment to refresh your memory about the seven life traps associated with women who are in love with men who "love" themselves. Remember, these life traps can be present in any combination.

Abandonment Life Trap: *You primarily feel rejection.*

Core belief: *People always leave you.*

Mistrust/Abuse Life Trap: *You feel hurt.*

Core belief: *People hurt or manipulate you.*

Emotional Deprivation Life Trap: *You feel misunderstood.*

Core belief: *No one is there for you.*

Defectiveness/Shame Life Trap: *You feel inadequate, unlovable, and unworthy.*

Core belief: *You are not good enough to love.*

Subjugation Life Trap: *You suppress your wants and needs in order to please someone else.*

Core belief: *If you don't meet someone else's needs, that person won't care about you. You don't have a choice.*

Self-Sacrifice Life Trap: *You feel responsible for others, feel guilty when you don't take care of others, but also feel resentment at taking care of others.*

Core belief: *You need to help or fix others, and it is your choice to do so.*

Unrelenting Standards Life Trap: *You feel the need to strive to be the best in everything, to be or have things be perfect, or to follow self-imposed rigid rules.*

Core belief: *Whatever you do, it will never be good enough.*

As you read about the various life traps originating in childhood, remember that you might recognize yourself in more than one. It is not uncommon to have more than one life trap. Also, life traps tend to overlap, so as you read through these children's experiences, note that they may have more than one life trap. Also, you may see similarities among the various stories. Certainly, the same child could have taken on a different life trap since they overlap. For example, someone who experienced emotional deprivation may also develop unrelenting standards to compensate for feelings of not being good enough. As you will learn in the next chapter, one or several of the life traps that caused you the most difficulty in childhood may recede as you become an adult while another of your childhood life traps takes center stage. For example, as a child you may have the life traps of emotional deprivation and unrelenting standards. In childhood, it's the emotional deprivation that is most difficult for you because your parents are not there for you; but in adulthood, the continual striving to meet your unrelenting standards may cause you the most problems because being a driven workaholic affects your health and your relationships.

As I mentioned earlier, I have included three vignettes for each of the seven life traps to illustrate how children may come from fairly different backgrounds but end up with the same life trap. Although these vignettes were all intended to be different, know that there is considerable overlap among the life traps. When you think of your own life traps, try to determine which one caused you the most difficulty in childhood.

Abandonment: Clare, Kirsten, and Lynette

The core belief with this life trap is that people always leave you. You struggled with separation more than other children because you experienced the loss of significant people in your life, most often a parent. The loss may have been due to a parent's emotional unavailability because of illness or a disability, or it may have been due to divorce or death.

Clare

Clare's parents led busy lives. Her father was a corporate executive for a large medical company and her mother was busy with charities and social events. Clare was cared for by nannies. The highlight of Clare's day was seeing her parents in the evening, even if only briefly. To compensate for their absence, her parents provided Clare and her brother with anything they wanted. When Clare was twelve, she was sent to boarding school. This was the norm in her family, since her parents had attended boarding schools when they were young. Clare was a sweet, sensitive, and shy little girl who did not want to leave home. But no matter how much she protested, her parents' decision was final.

Clare developed severe diarrhea on her first day of boarding school after her parents left her. Soon she was struggling with chronic diarrhea after every holiday or home visit. In summers, Clare was sent to camps. Clare continued to beg her parents not to leave her. Although Clare's parents thought they were doing the best for her, they unknowingly set her up with a core belief that the people she loved would leave her.

Kirsten

Kirsten's father was an alcoholic who beat her mother when he drank. More than once Kirsten witnessed her father point a gun at her mother and threaten to shoot her. Her mother would yell back, "Go on, kill me!" Kirsten watched in horror, silently screaming for her mother to shut up. Kirsten was terrified her mother would be killed, her father would be hauled off to jail, and she would be left alone. Every time her parents fought, she felt as if her world might end. Her home life was in constant chaos. Kristen was anxious and frightened that she would be left alone.

Lynette

Lynette's mother had severe depression. Lynette remembers banging on her mother's locked bedroom door, crying and begging her mother to open the door to no avail. Lynnette said she felt "terror and then helplessness" every time her mother started down the hall to her bedroom. The helplessness turned into resignation once it was clear her mother was not coming out. Lynette would get herself breakfast, get dressed, and get herself off to school. But she ultimately developed into an anxious, clingy child who had difficulty with any kind of endings or separations.

Mistrust and Abuse: Monica, Maggie, and Kelli

The core belief with this life trap is that people who are supposed to love and take care of you actually hurt or manipulate you. Some children with this life trap come to believe they caused the problem, so they deserve to be abused or mistreated. Of course, this is *never* true. It is never your fault if you were abused. Abuse, however, is not the only source of mistrust. Children can also develop mistrust if they have overprotective parents who give them the message that the world is not safe.

Monica

Monica was seven and her sister was five. An older male cousin, seventeen, lived nearby with their aunt. Since Monica's parents worked all day, the cousin was paid to watch them after school. Instead of watching them, he beat them. He made them be his "slaves" and ordered them around: make food, bring drinks, stand next to the TV ready to change the channel—anything he ordered. They were at his beck and call, and if they disagreed, he would hit them. His beatings were what Monica feared most. If she tried to hide under the bed, he would pull her out by her hair. He liked it when she tried to hide, and he enjoyed chasing, catching, and then beating her. Sometimes when she was about to be beaten, she would "float away" in her mind. He told her she could never tell her parents or he'd hurt her dog. Monica could not concentrate at school, knowing what was waiting for her at home. She began having stomachaches at school and spent hours lying on the bed in the nurse's office with a hot water bottle. Still she never told anyone. Her cousin didn't stop until her family moved out of state when she was ten. Monica did not trust others and felt helpless to protect herself from others' abuse, so she did not develop close relationships.

Maggie

Maggie had a slight hearing problem as a child. Her family teased her incessantly about the fact that she had to ask "What?" all the time. They called her stupid. Sometimes they talked softly on purpose just so she would have to say "What?" and then they could ridicule her. They did this often in front of family or friends. If she got upset, she was accused of over-reacting. When she tried to get her mother to intervene, she was told it was all in fun and that she was too sensitive. Maggie became very self-conscious about her hearing problem. She tried to hide it at school by not getting close to others, not asking "What?", and nodding her head in agreement when others talked to her. She lived in fear of being humiliated in front of her peers. She never brought friends home for fear her family would make fun of her. Maggie came to expect that everyone would make fun of her.

Kelli

Kelli's parents were overprotective. As a very young child, she was not given the opportunity to explore her world without her mother's watchful eyes. Her parents made her believe that the world was not a safe place. She was told that only her family and the church were safe and could be trusted. Her mother's answer to everything was in the Bible. Her parents homeschooled her to keep her safe from the dangerous world. She was told that people are out to take advantage of you and that she would not be able to tell the ones who wanted to take advantage of her from the ones who didn't. Kelli became mistrustful and afraid of everything and everyone outside her family or church.

Mistrust and Abuse Quiz

Answer the following questions about these children.

1. Who uses the coping style of avoidance?

2. Who do you think has the most shame about herself as an adult?

(Compare your answers with the answers at the end of the chapter.)

Emotional Deprivation: Anita, Kathryn, and Vivienne

The core belief of this life trap is "no one is there for me." These children feel that something is missing, and they are right. Quite often, they are missing nurturance, love, understanding, empathy, guidance, and/or protection. Because of this they feel lonely and misunderstood. They have a sense of emptiness and a belief that they will always be alone.

Anita

Anita was the baby of the family. She had three older brothers. When Anita was born, her mother adored her. She had always wanted a girl and was thrilled when she had Anita. She dressed Anita up in pretty dresses and showed her off to everyone. Anita became a very attractive little girl, and her mother loved hearing, from family as well as strangers, how beautiful her daughter was. But as Anita became older, her mother's adoration never progressed beyond dressing her up and showing her off. Anita craved something more but wasn't sure what that was. Even when her mother hugged her, she felt as if something was missing. Anita's mother was never able to "see" Anita beyond her physical appearance. Anita grew up feeling her mother never really knew or understood her, or really cared about her. Her mother dismissed any of Anita's ideas, wants, and desires, if they weren't in line with her own.

When the family moved to a new house, Anita asked to have her room painted lilac. Her mother detested that color and made Anita have a pale yellow room, the color she liked. Anita wanted to play the flute, but her mother insisted Anita play the piano because she played the piano. When Anita protested, her mother flew into a rage and accused Anita of being an ungrateful brat. Anita had a lot of frustration and anger at her mother. She wouldn't back down, but she also never got her way. They fought all the time. Anita became defensive with everyone—siblings, school friends, and teachers. And she came to believe that she would always have to fight to get her needs met. She assumed no one would ever understand her.

Kathryn

Kathryn grew up in a rural area, the youngest of five children. Her father was a hard worker, and her mother took in laundry. By the time Kathryn came along, her mother was worn out and tired. Her two parents provided a home for their children, but little else. Her parents had not gone past the sixth grade in their education, so they put no emphasis on education for their children. But Kathryn was a curious child who liked to learn. No one in her family understood or could appreciate her love of books and learning. There was no enrichment provided for her curiosity. Kathryn often felt deeply lonely. She said she would sit on her bed, look out the window at the empty fields next door, and think, *Something is missing.* Kathryn came to believe she would always feel empty, lonely, and misunderstood.

Vivienne

Vivienne's mother was cold and detached. Try as Vivienne might to engage with her mother, she couldn't do it. Her mother was not interested in anything Vivienne said or did, yet Vivienne still tried to be near her. She loved to go into her mother's bedroom, sit quietly on her bed, and watch her mother put on makeup and get dressed. She thought her mother was beautiful. Her mother, irritated at her presence, would tell her to leave because she was in the way as she was trying to get ready. Her mother was divorced but dated frequently. She put her boyfriends ahead of her children. Vivienne and her siblings were left to fend for themselves while their mother went on dates. Her mother would leave them a blank check to order dinner with. Vivienne does not recall having even one dinner together as a family. She grew up eating fast food. She comforted herself with food, trying to fill the emptiness inside of her. Yet her mother portrayed the family as perfect, showing everyone pictures of all the places she took them. Her mother had inherited money from her family. She bought the children lavish gifts and took them on vacations but didn't spend time with them. Vivienne felt unloved and lonely and came to expect that no one would ever love her and that she would ultimately always be alone.

Emotional Deprivation Quiz

Answer the following questions about these children.

1. Who do you think uses surrender as a coping style?

2. Who is likely to end up with an eating problem as an adult?

(Compare your answers with the answers at the end of the chapter.)

Defectiveness: Pat, Kimberly, and Trisha

Children with this life trap believe they are never good enough to love. They feel inadequate and unworthy of love. They believe this is because something is wrong with them. They are somehow defective. Defectiveness is different from emotional deprivation, in which the child believes the problem is with others outside of him or her, such as a parent. With defectiveness, the child believes the problem lies within, that he or she is defective.

Pat

Pat grew up in a home with a highly critical mother. She was made to feel she was never good enough. Her mother's disappointment with her was obvious through grimaces and sighs. Pat's mother was appearance conscious, and she could not understand why her daughter was not. Pat, unlike her showy, ladylike mother, was a tomboy and preferred playing outside in the woods to having a tea party with dolls. As a result of her mother's constant criticisms and obvious disappointment with her, Pat became self-conscious and shy. One time Pat's mother called her in from playing outside. To Pat's horror, her mother told her she looked like an animal the way she was running around outside. Then her mother imitated a loping animal. She said Pat was the joke of the neighborhood. Pat felt the heat of shame fill her face. Pat was never able to accept compliments. If someone complimented her, she thought they were secretly making fun of her, or it was a joke that she would be the butt of. She was insecure, with no self-confidence. She felt inadequate and unworthy of love.

Kimberly

Kimberly was nine when a family friend who rented a room in their house came into her bedroom one night. She did not understand what was happening. Afterward he told her that her parents would be very mad at her if they knew what she did and that they would likely send her away. He assured her they would no longer love her. She was told she had to keep it a secret. She did.

Her mother was a nurse who worked nights, and the family needed the income a night shift paid. Her father, a truck driver, was absent for long periods of time. Her parents' bedroom was on the main level of the house and Kimberly's was on the upper level. Her parents never suspected.

She often hoped her mother would somehow just know. She thought she was giving them hints: her appetite decreased, even for her favorite desserts; her grades slipped; and she was sassy and irritable. Her family didn't seem to notice. No one suspected sexual abuse, not even her pediatrician. When her mother talked to him about her decreased appetite and weight loss, he said it was a phase that she would grow out of and not to worry. Kimberly's frustration and irritability eventually turned to despair. Kimberly did not feel safe in the house. She did not know how to protect herself from the abuse. Her parents, who should have provided safety and protection for her, had no idea their daughter was being abused under their roof. But as the abuse continued, Kimberly felt less and less worthy of their love. Shame engulfed her. She became withdrawn. When she started her menses, the family friend abruptly stopped coming into her bedroom. She was relieved but was still left with a secret. Even after he moved out, she could not shake the feeling of shame and even disgust with herself. She came to believe that somehow she was fundamentally bad for this to have happened to her. She never told her parents or anyone. Kimberly, believing she was defective, lived silently with her shame.

Trisha

Trisha never knew her father because he left the family when she was a baby. As the family story goes, she was a colicky baby who cried nonstop. Her father was hotheaded and impatient and couldn't take the crying. He'd be irritable and yell at her mother and two older siblings, telling them to shut Trisha up. Her mother, afraid he might finally hit the baby, protected her by taking her into the basement. Trisha's father threatened to leave if the baby was not shut up. The family could not afford to have him leave. It threatened their very existence since he was the sole bread-winner, albeit not very successful. He was a laborer but could never hold on to a steady job because of his temper. Her mother never finished high school because she had become pregnant with their first child. Although Trisha's mother tried to get her to stop crying, she continued for almost fourteen weeks. It was toward the end of this time that her father left, and it sent the family into a tailspin.

Trisha's mother became distraught, and the other children became sad and angry. The family had to go on welfare. Trisha's older siblings were embarrassed to get groceries from the food pantries, holiday meals at churches, and clothes from Goodwill or Salvation Army. The siblings blamed the baby. By the time Trisha was old enough to understand what had happened, she was told it was her fault their father had left and the family had been thrown into poverty. She grew up believing it was her fault and having it confirmed at every turn by her siblings' anger toward her and by the family's financial difficulties. She felt guilt and shame about the way they lived, and she blamed herself for it. She also felt there must be something horribly wrong with her for her father to leave, besides her colic as a baby. She would wonder, *It couldn't have been just because I was crying, could it?*

Defectiveness Quiz

Answer the following questions about these children.

1. Who do you think will accept abuse from others as an adult?

2. Who will be unable to recognize the signs of sincere people as an adult?

(Compare your answers with the answers at the end of the chapter.)

Subjugation: Alice, Petra, and Marty

The core belief of this life trap is that if you don't meet the needs of others, they won't love or care about you. Children with this life trap put other people's needs ahead of their own. They feel they don't have a choice. They may feel trapped and oppressed. These children experience love as conditional on their meeting their parents' wants and desires. Not meeting their parents' wants and desires results in love being withheld. These children may become hypervigilant to the wants and needs of others. They can become people pleasers.

Alice

Alice was a quiet, kind, and sensitive little girl. Her mother was a strong woman who knew exactly what she wanted and how she wanted it, and she made sure she got it. As long as Alice agreed with her mother, everything was fine, but if she disagreed, she would be met with her mother's anger or a withdrawal of her mother's affection. Alice loved her mother and craved her mother's approval. So she learned early in life that it was better to give up what she wanted and have a mother who adored her than to argue for her own needs and lose her mother's affection. When Alice was among friends, she went along with whatever they wanted. She never offered a different suggestion or opinion. Alice was very well liked by her peers and by her teachers. Alice worried a great deal about what others thought of her or if she had offended anyone.

Petra

Petra was raised in a strict religious family. She was indoctrinated to believe that being selfless was a virtue. Asserting your own desires, wants, and needs was being selfish. Her mother was considered a saint and a martyr at their church. Her father insisted the family attend church three times a week in addition to all day Sunday. The Bible was considered the only book worthy of reading. The children were not allowed to watch TV, dance, or read popular books or magazines. Forget the Internet. Petra went to a small school with other children from her church. If she ever complained or, worse, questioned her father's authority, she was severely scolded and told she was ungrateful and selfish. Petra loved art. She drew all the time but kept her drawings hidden after her father found one and ripped it up, calling it frivolous and not doing God's work. Petra felt oppressed by her father's dictatorial ways. She did not think she had a choice in the matter. Petra came to believe she was selfish if she asserted her needs. She felt obligated to put others' needs ahead of her own.

Marty

Marty was a twin who was raised in a loving but strict family. Her parents did not have children until they were older. Her mother was twenty-eight and her father was forty-four when they married. Her mother was a real estate broker, and her father was a career military man. He believed in corporal punishment. As a young child, she dared not go against him because she had been spanked more than once. She always tried to be good to avoid his anger, which she interpreted as him not loving her anymore. Her father retired when Marty was in high school. After that, he became more controlling. He wanted to know her every move. She had to check in with him whenever she went out with friends or on a date. One time she missed curfew by a couple minutes and her father took away her driving privileges for two weeks. Many times Marty was frustrated with the level of control her father imposed on her. She felt stifled and resented it, but he had the power, not her, so there was nothing she could do about it. Marty avoided conflict with everyone.

Subjugation Quiz

Answer the following questions about these children.

1. Who do you think will become the biggest people pleaser as an adult?

2. Who is most likely to have problems with authority figures as an adult?

(Compare your answers with the answers at the end of the chapter.)

Self-Sacrifice: Dianne, Marlene, and Lily

The core belief of this life trap is that you need to help or fix others. You feel it is your responsibility. Children with this life trap are very sensitive to the feelings of others. They can't stand to see others in pain or suffering, emotionally or physically. They are so devoted to helping others that they put their own needs last. At times, they may resent putting their needs last, but then they feel guilty for thinking this way, so they ignore their feeling of resentment. Self-sacrifice differs from subjugation in that with self-sacrifice you make the choice to put the needs of others ahead of your own, whereas with subjugation you believe you don't have a choice. In other words, subjugation feels involuntary and self-sacrifice is voluntary.

Dianne

Dianne was eleven when her mother was diagnosed with multiple sclerosis (MS). She had three younger siblings. Dianne had always been sensitive and caring about others. As her mother's condition grew worse, Dianne pitched in more to help out. She loved her mother and wanted her mother to live the best life she could. Her father, normally a great dad, was unable to face the diagnosis of his wife. He was out of the house as much as possible, working or whatever. Dianne began taking on more and more of the household responsibilities: making dinner, cleaning, helping her siblings get off to school, helping with their homework, and getting them bathed and to bed. By the time she was in high school, she had no life of her own. She didn't join any after-school activities and never dated because she had to come home and help her mother. Her father seemed complacent with this arrangement. Occasionally, Dianne resented her mother for having MS, and for all the childhood and adolescent things she had to forgo, but then she felt guilty, knowing it wasn't her mother's fault. In all relationships, Dianne came to feel guilty if she put herself first.

Marlene

Marlene's father died of a sudden heart attack in his early forties. Her mother became sad and depressed. Marlene hated to see her mother unhappy. She wanted more than anything to take away her mother's pain. Although Marlene was only eleven, she stepped in as her mother's confidante and surrogate partner. Marlene sat with her mother for hours when she grieved, listened to her fears and concerns, encouraged her when it was time to look for a job, and accompanied her to places when she didn't want to go alone. Marlene knew she was a huge help to her mother at this difficult time, and that made her feel good. Marlene never thought about the fact that she also suffered a loss when her father died. Her focus was only on her mother's pain and grief, not her own. Whenever she began to feel sad or resentful, she reassured herself that she was a good daughter. Besides, helping others was a virtue.

Lily

Lily had a younger brother who was born with achondroplasia, a form of dwarfism. He had multiple surgeries and a lot of health problems. Lily's father was an alcoholic who couldn't handle having a child with special needs, and he couldn't accept his son's condition. He argued often with her mother, fueled by his alcohol consumption. After he divorced her mother, Lily rarely saw her father. Her mother had a difficult time adjusting to being alone and managing everything without her husband. She had always been dependent on her husband to handle everything. When he left, she became overwhelmed and helpless. This is where Lily stepped in. Seeing her mother's difficult adjustment, she took it upon herself to assume as much responsibility around the house as she could in order to lessen the burden on her mother. She felt sorry for her mother but also worried her mother might leave, too, if she became overwhelmed. So Lily cleaned the house, did laundry, and fixed simple meals. She'd get up early to fix breakfast and feed and dress her brother. Taking care of things to ease her mother's burden assured Lily of her mother's presence. Lily's mother always promised to help more the next day, but she never kept her promise. Sometimes Lily would get annoyed at her mother for not keeping her promise and for not being the mom. But she didn't like feeling that way because it reminded her of her father's anger. At these times, Lily would try harder to be compassionate toward her mother and do more around the house. Lily came to believe that it was her duty to help others and to ease their burdens. She also believed if she did not help others, she would lose a loved one. Lily became the child who was first to volunteer to help in any situation. To that end, she would work tirelessly and not complain. But she was never comfortable accepting help from others.

Self-Sacrifice Quiz

Answer the following questions about these children.

1. Who will have codependency behaviors as an adult?

2. Who uses surrender as a coping style?

(Compare your answers with the answers at the end of the chapter.)

Unrelenting Standards: Jennifer, Chelsea, and Elspeth

The core belief of this life trap is that whatever you do, it's never good enough. People with this life trap are successful, but they always feel they could have done better. They are constantly striving to meet their unrealistic expectations, and they get mad at themselves when they don't. These children always feel pressure to perform and attain their goals, but they feel there is never enough time. The unrelenting standards life trap differs from the defectiveness life trap in that children with the defectiveness life trap feel they are unworthy and therefore not good enough to be loved or valued. Children with the unrelenting standards life trap know they're okay; they just think they could do or be better at whatever they are striving to achieve. Schema theory has identified three types of unrelenting standards: achievement oriented (workaholic), status oriented (need to have or be the best of/at everything), and compulsivity (slave to perfection and perfect order). The following vignettes are examples of each type.

Jennifer: Oriented to Achievement

Jennifer grew up with a father who made it clear that there was no room for mistakes. If she didn't keep her room in perfect order, he called her lazy and expressed his deep disappointment in her. If she didn't get an A on an exam, he would angrily accuse her of not having tried her best and then lecture her on the merits of trying one's best. He would tell her that if she couldn't do it now, as a child, she would never succeed later in life, and then he would paint a very bleak picture of her future. She loved her father more than anyone and wanted his approval more than anything. The *only* time she ever received attention or praise from him was when she won an award or achieved some accomplishment. At those times, it was bliss. He was so affectionate and happy with her. Jennifer became very anxious as a child, fearful of not living up to her father's expectations of her. She put so much pressure on herself to achieve and live up to his expectations that she developed terrible headaches and later migraines.

Chelsea: Oriented to Status

Chelsea grew up in a family in which money and status were important. Her mother was on the board of many charitable organizations. Her father was a prominent surgeon. Their home was a showplace. It was built by a famous architect and decorated by the best designer in the area. Having the best of everything and being the best at everything was expected and taken for granted. Because Chelsea's parents cared so much about status and wealth, Chelsea adopted these values. She was driven toward achieving recognition and attaining status in everything she did.

Chelsea loved horses and riding. Her parents bought her a horse that most adults would envy. Chelsea rode at the premier barn with the best instructor money could buy, and she insisted on having the best riding clothes and tack. She wore a Rolex and only felt good about herself if she wore the most current designer clothes. When she was a senior in high school, she got a Lexus SUV. Her freshman year of college, Chelsea found the most prestigious sorority with girls from the "best" families to assure that she'd meet the most eligible men. Chelsea was not taking any chances. She sought out and befriended girls already in the sorority and made sure they knew about her volunteer activities on campus and her accomplishments over the summer. Her work paid off, and she was asked to join the sorority. Attaining more status symbols was never ending. There was always something more, something better that she needed in order to feel good enough. This feeling drove her to constantly strive to attain more recognition and status.

Elspeth: Oriented to Compulsivity

As a result of her childhood experiences, Elspeth became compulsivity oriented. Elspeth's father was a partner in a prestigious law firm, and her mother was the head of a national nonprofit. They expected their children to adhere to their high standards. The children were on a tight schedule and their parents expected them to follow it. The house was immaculate and was to stay that way. Elspeth was expected to keep her room in perfect order. One of Elspeth's earliest memories is of arranging and rearranging her stuffed animals on her bed, trying to get them just right. She also learned to color by outlining the picture first and then filling in the color. She got upset with herself if she went outside the lines.

She was never satisfied with anything she did. If she made a minor mistake or one little thing was out of order, she focused on that, not the fact that she had just accomplished something brilliant. Once, in grade school, she scored the majority of the points in a soccer game but missed one goal. Her team still won. Rather than enjoying the win and her excellent performance, she could not stop berating herself for missing that one goal. When the team was celebrating afterward, she could not feel good about herself because she had let herself down. The next day she went out early to the field and practiced for hours in an effort to not miss a goal the next time. In everything she did, Elspeth compulsively focused on any small detail she missed.

Unrelenting Standards Quiz

Answer the following questions about these children.

1. Who do you think feels the most emotionally empty?

2. Who is the perfectionist?

(Compare your answers with the answers at the end of the chapter.)

I hope that by reading these vignettes you now have a better understanding of how childhood wounding manifests in the seven life traps and how children from varied backgrounds can have the same life trap. Did you see yourself in one or more of these life traps? Now that you have read through these vignettes, get out your journal and complete the following exercise.

Exercise 4: *Origins of Your Childhood Life Traps*

Review the life trap vignettes above and record in your journal which life trap felt most relevant to you as a child. Think back to when you were a child and how you thought and felt then, not how you view your childhood today from an adult perspective. Record the childhood experiences that caused your life trap and answer these questions:

- What core beliefs did you come to hold about yourself?

- What role did shame and vulnerability play in your childhood and in the development of your core belief(s)?

- Which coping style—overcompensation, surrender, or avoidance—did you use most often and when (for example, at home, at school, and so on)? Consider why you opted for this coping style. In other words, how did that coping style fit with your personality?

- What, if any, codependent behaviors did you display as a child?

If you found this useful for your primary life trap, answer these questions for the other life traps you selected as well. Write your responses in your journal.

Exercise 5: *Write a Childhood Narrative*

In your journal, write your own childhood narrative (one to three paragraphs) from your perspective as a child. (Use the bulleted items below to organize your narrative.) It's important that you stick with your perspective as child: For example, let's say you suffered the life trap of emotional deprivation as a child. You may want to say, "Because I was the youngest of seven, my mom struggled to give me attention. After all, she must have felt overwhelmed with all those demands. She just didn't have time." Instead, connect with how it felt to you as a child. For example, "When my mother gave attention to my other siblings, I felt left out, sad, and jealous all at once. I wanted her to hold me like she held and comforted my siblings." (In addition to writing from your perspective as a child, when you consider the following, you can write about a parent or any *primary* caregiver, such as a grandparent, an aunt, or a neighbor—whoever had the most influence in your life as a child.)

- *Describe your relationship with each of your parents.* Was one missing due to death or a divorce? What adjectives would you use to describe each of your parents? Caring, cold, uninterested, giving, trying? Remember, stay in your child! It can be very tempting to cut them slack because we may have developed empathy for their job as parents as we matured.

- *Choose one or two childhood experiences that stick out in your memory.* Usually these are significant, something like "I came home from school and told my mother about a mean thing a kid did to me and all she could say was, 'What did you do to make that kid mad at you?' I felt misunderstood and unjustly accused."

- *Think of how you managed your painful feelings.* Did you use one of the coping styles? Was one more prominent than others? Did you use more than one?

Exercise 6: *Key Words*

If you'd rather not write out a narrative, jot down in your journal some key words that describe your situation and you as a child—for example, lonely, unhappy, miserable, fearful, and so on. Follow the italicized prompts in Exercise 5.

Exercise 7: *Complete the Sentence*

If you'd rather, write the phrases below in your journal and then complete each sentence to reflect what you wish your parents had been like.

- I wanted my mother to…

    OR let your child speak directly to your primary caregiver, for example,

- "Mommy, I want you to…"

    Ask yourself if there is a deeper layer to your answer. For example, at first, you might say you wanted your mother's *attention*, but the deeper layer was that you wanted your mother's *affection*.

Putting It All Together

In this chapter, we focused on childhood life traps and the various ways in which these life traps can be manifested depending on life circumstances and the makeup of the individual child. You also had the opportunity to consider your own core beliefs and life traps that developed out of your childhood wounding, as well as corresponding feelings, coping styles, and behaviors. In the next chapter, vignettes will reveal what childhood life traps look like in adulthood and how shame, vulnerability, coping styles, and codependency from your childhood can affect your adult dating choices and relationships.

Answers to the Quizzes:

Abandonment

1. Clare (fought to stay home)
2. Lynette (already clingy)

Mistrust and Abuse

1. Monica ("floats away")
2. Maggie (due to her family's teasing about her hearing)

Emotional Deprivation

1. Kathryn (accepted her circumstances) and Vivienne (accepted she would not be loved)
2. Vivienne (uses food as a comfort)

Defectiveness

1. Kimberly (was abused; felt powerless and helpless)
2. Pat (cannot accept compliments)

Subjugation

1. Alice (worried about what others think of her)
2. Marty (resented her father's control)

Self-Sacrifice

1. All three
2. All three

Unrelenting Standards

1. Chelsea (only has status and things, no emotional connections to others)
2. Elspeth (never satisfied, notices every little mistake)

CHAPTER 5

Stuck for Life?
Your Life Traps in Adulthood

Are you "stuck for life"? Your childhood experiences gave rise to core beliefs, which in turn resulted in your specific life traps. You carried these life traps into adulthood. They are etched in your psyche by your core beliefs. The problem is that your life traps are no longer helpful, but you are unaware of it. To you, they are just the normal ways you think and behave in the world. They are as natural to you as breathing. This is why you may not recognize a narcissist partner and why you keep ending up in destructive, unhealthy, narcissistic relationships. You may blame yourself for being stupid because you keep picking narcissistic men, when in truth it's not your fault. You did not cause the negative childhood experiences that shaped your patterns of thinking and behaving. You were doing the best you could to survive. I wrote this book to help you stop blaming yourself for repeating narcissistic relationships and learn about the forces that have been in your driver's seat. It's time to take the wheel back and steer your own course, one that will take you along the path toward a healthy relationship. Let's start.

Essential Elements

This chapter focuses on how your childhood life traps are manifested in adulthood and how they impact your dating choices. We'll revisit the children presented in the vignettes in chapter 4 as adults to see how their childhood wounding shows up in their adult lives. Some childhood life traps remain prominent in adulthood whereas others recede. Also, you'll see how shame, vulnerability, coping styles, and codependency carry through from childhood into adulthood, affecting your dating choices and relationships.

Adult Life Traps

You will now see how each of the girls in the childhood vignettes from chapter 4 fared in adulthood. Even though they had different childhood experiences, they all became susceptible to the charms of narcissistic partners in adulthood. These women were attracted to narcissistic men because the men met their need to compensate for negative feelings about themselves, feelings that stemmed from their childhood experiences. Let's look at each of these girls, now grown up, and their dating choices.

Abandonment: Clare, Kirsten, and Lynette

Women who had the life trap of abandonment in childhood have this core belief: *people always leave me.* As adults, they are attracted to men who make them feel secure. Narcissistic men home in on women's needs like a laser beam. They make you believe they will keep you safe and secure and never leave you. But once they have you, their true colors emerge, and it's too late. Terrified of being abandoned, you desperately cling to the unhealthy, destructive narcissistic relationship.

Clare

Clare's Childhood Coping Styles: Overcompensation and avoidance

Clare's Childhood: Clare was from a privileged family and never had to worry about anything, but her parents were not around. She was sent away to boarding school against her wishes.

Clare's Adulthood: Clare was naïve, especially when it came to men. She had a series of boyfriends in college, all of whom were cads. She was attracted to showboat guys, probably because she was so insecure about herself, but they were not the type to settle down. Her clinginess caused them to leave her. At a sorority event in college, she met the man who was to be her future husband. He was a confident, take-charge man. She was immediately attracted to him. He was charming and sophisticated, and she knew he would be successful. She thought he could take care of her as her father always had. They dated, but every time he was away from her, she panicked, worried he would meet someone else or something terrible would happen to him. She insisted he call her the minute he arrived at his destination. Once he left, he usually forgot he'd promised to call, but her frantic texts or calls reminded him, and he resented the intrusions on his time. He often responded in a curt manner. If he couldn't explain his time away from her, fear got the best of her, and she'd accuse him of seeing another woman. He would then accuse her of being petty and jealous.

Clare clung to him, and they eventually married. She was miserable in the marriage. He was often aloof and dismissive. He traveled a lot for his work, and she continued to worry something terrible would happen to him. When she found out he was having an affair, she was beside herself, but her fear of losing him proved too strong. She forgave him when he apologized and put up with his cheating behaviors for years. After twenty-two years of marriage, he divorced her for a newer model. She was devastated.

Kirsten

Kirsten's Childhood Coping Style: Surrender

Kirsten's Childhood: Her father was an alcoholic and not available for days on end. She had an unstable childhood; no one was there for her. Her father beat her mother, and then almost killed her, waving a gun at her while Kirsten watched, terrified of losing them both. Kirsten could not wait to get away from her family.

Kirsten's Adulthood: Kirsten married the first boy she met just to get out of the house. She wasn't in love with him. He was like a big kid. Even after they'd been married for years and had children, he still hung out with the guys, drinking and watching sports on the weekends. He'd come home drunk and pass out in the living room. When he was hungover the next day, he didn't help with the kids or chores. Although Kirsten was unhappy, there was something familiar in his unpredictability and drinking. As much as she hated her husband's behaviors, she could not bring herself to leave him. She could not imagine being on her own, even though she had a well-paying job. She continued to deny how bad it was. She realized her denial had started years before when he didn't show up for the birth of their first baby. He was on a fishing trip, which he would not cancel even though it overlapped with her due date. He told her he knew she would be brave, and he would make it up to her when he returned.

After that, nothing changed in their marriage. She was unhappy but would not let herself think about it. She had anxiety and suffered from irritable bowel syndrome (IBS). When her IBS flared up, she would be hospitalized, but she could still not face the idea of losing her marriage and being alone. She considered having another child, hoping that would keep her husband in the marriage.

Lynette

Lynette's Childhood Coping Styles: Surrender, avoidance, and overcompensation

Lynette's Childhood: Lynette grew up with a mother who had severe depression. Her mother would take to her bed for days in a row, lock her door, and be unavailable to her daughter.

Lynette's Adulthood: When Lynette was twenty-eight, she met a man who was thirty-one. She ignored the red flags that he still lived at home with his mother and had never had a full- or even part-time job for more than three weeks. He was always being fired for tardiness or not showing up at all. He'd tell Lynette his boss was a jerk and had it in for him. He never took responsibility. Lynette accepted his excuses. He could become verbally abusive, and he knew which of her vulnerabilities to attack. She knew the relationship was not good for her, and her friends and family told her that all the time, but she talked herself into the idea that maybe it was her fault. After all, everything he said about her had a kernel of truth—just enough for her to doubt herself. Also, if the problem was within her, she could fix that. She spent a lot of time reading books, exercising, and dieting. She stopped telling her friends about how he treated her. She was ashamed that she took his abuse and could not leave him.

Their relationship was like a roller coaster ride over which she had no control. They would be getting along when out of the blue he would start complaining about her in a hurtful way, knowing it would make her panic. At the height of her panic, he would tell her they needed to separate. He sadistically enjoyed watching her crumble. Then she would beg him to take her back. After she groveled enough, accepting all the blame for his unhappiness, he reluctantly would take her back, and it would start over again.

Your Looking Glass

Before we go on, take a moment to reflect on what you've read so far about these three women. Do you recognize yourself in their stories? Notice how you are feeling emotionally and physically. What thoughts are going through your head *right now*? Write them in your journal.

Abandonment Quiz

Check the box (or boxes) that identify which coping style is still prominent in adulthood for Clare, Kirsten, and Lynette.

	Overcompensation	Avoidance	Surrender
Clare	☐	☐	☐
Kirsten	☐	☐	☐
Lynette	☐	☐	☐

Now pull out your journal and jot a few notes about Clare, Kirsten, and Lynette. Where do you see their coping style(s) at work in their lives?

(Answers are at the end of the chapter.)

Mistrust/Abuse: Monica, Maggie, and Kelli

Women who had the life trap of mistrust/abuse in childhood have this core belief: *people hurt or manipulate me*. These women are attracted to narcissistic men whom they mistakenly believe can be trusted not to hurt or abuse them. These women are powerless to leave the narcissist when he becomes emotionally and/or physically abusive because his behavior fits with their core belief that people hurt or manipulate them and/or that they deserve it.

Monica

Monica's Childhood Coping Style: Avoidance

Monica's Childhood: Monica's male cousin was physically abusive. Monica feared coming home from school. She never told her parents.

Monica's Adulthood: Monica was hypervigilant about everything in her environment. She paid attention to people's body language, eye contact, and voice. This was especially true when she dated men. She never seemed to be able to relax on a date, and it didn't make for an enjoyable evening.

All her dates seemed to be with angry, vindictive men who demanded respect from everyone but rarely gave it. One time her date became angry and raised his voice with the parking valet. He then tried to get the valet fired. Another date criticized the kid behind the popcorn counter at a movie because he was too slow. He heckled this kid while waiting in line. Monica was embarrassed as people turned and stared at them. In time, every man she dated would eventually start to criticize her. They often flew into a rage if she protested and smashed something valuable of hers or took away a planned event, like a dinner. Dating became increasingly difficult as Monica came to believe men were all the same: volatile, mean, and vindictive. Her dates would say things that made her think they might be abusive, and she'd be gone. Eventually, she made the decision not to date. She assumed she would be alone and preferred it that way rather than risk being in what she expected—another abusive relationship with a jerk.

Maggie

Maggie's Childhood Coping Style: Avoidance

Maggie's Childhood: Maggie had a slight hearing problem growing up. Her family teased her about it. If she complained, they told her she was overreacting. Maggie became self-conscious and wouldn't bring friends home for fear of being teased.

Maggie's Adulthood: By the time Maggie was an adult, her hearing problem had resolved, but Maggie had become a people pleaser. As a librarian, she had to be part of a team as well as work with an administration. Interpersonal interactions were always difficult for her, but she found being agreeable with others worked for her. Maggie started dating a salesman. He had a wonderful personality and lots of friends, unlike the silent broody types she had dated in the past. She was immediately attracted to him and couldn't believe her good fortune that such a really cool guy liked her. For the first time, she felt good about herself. She felt proud being seen with him. But sometimes he teased her in a way that stirred up feelings from her childhood. He teased her about how she pronounced certain words, a residual artifact from her childhood hearing problem. She could not pronounce the word "Nicaragua" clearly and he loved for her to say it so he could tease her. He teased her about other things she enjoyed, such as books, movies, and hobbies. His teasing felt like a personal attack. If she reacted to his teasing, he'd take offense and withdraw by giving her the silent treatment. She'd apologize for being so sensitive. She was eager to please him in any way, and he took advantage of it.

She married him and, in time, her self-worth became contingent on his approval. When he was in a good mood, she felt great about herself, but when he was in one of his critical moods, she felt worthless. His teasing eventually expanded outside their home. At dinners with friends, he brought up her faults as if they were endearing to him, but it hurt her feelings. If she brought it up on the way home, he would say he was disgusted with her immature ways, calling her a child and saying that he didn't know why he stayed with her. He'd compare her to women he worked with, asking her why she couldn't be more like them—more mature, intelligent, and sexy. He even wondered aloud how one of them would be in bed. If she expressed jealousy, he would criticize her for being jealous, saying that he was only thinking out loud. Maggie tried harder to please him. She bought sexy lingerie and agreed to watch porn with him, even though she didn't like it. Little by little, her self-esteem was eroded by his cruel emotional abuse. Eventually, she didn't recognize herself. Maggie was gone, and in her place was a shadow of a woman devoted to pleasing a cruel man.

Kelli

Kelli's Childhood Coping Style: Surrender

Kelli's Childhood: Her parents were very overprotective. They made her feel and believe that the world was not a safe place.

Kelli's Adulthood: As an adult, Kelli was fearful of everything, but when it came to men, she found herself attracted to men who were in positions of power and authority. In college, she was attracted to her professors and later, her bosses at work. Kelli believed in the sanctity of marriage and not having sex before she was married. When her boss, to whom she was strongly attracted, asked her out, she could not say no. She was completely intoxicated by his suave demeanor. They dated secretly to avoid "an office scandal." In truth, it was because he was just ending another affair with another woman in the office. Kelli had no idea. Although she had never done anything outside her values, she could not help herself now. When he touched her breasts for the first time, she felt electrified. He pushed her to have sex. She kept refusing, but after a short while, she couldn't refuse. Sex with him was amazing. For the first time, she was emotionally and physically in love with a man. Soon he asked her to do sexual things she had never heard of before. Kelli was uncomfortable and embarrassed, but she went along with him. He was her protector, and she felt safe with him.

Eventually, he asked her to do work for him on the side and paid her cash for services. He also paid for everything they ever did together. Many times he would hand her a fifty-dollar bill and smile. He then took her to swinging groups where he just asked her to watch. But soon he was asking her to have sex with other men so he could have sex with other women. She complied, all the while uncomfortable.

Soon he started to become distant. No matter what Kelli did to engage him, he was uninterested. She feared she was boring to him, with nothing of value to offer. When he became distant at work, she became afraid. Her protector was no longer there for her. She felt very vulnerable. When she questioned him, he broke it off and became hostile at work. Kelli knew she should quit, but she was helpless to do so. She just endured his abuse at work. Soon she could see he was into another woman in the company. Kelli felt used and discarded, like a used piece of tissue. She couldn't stop comparing herself to his new girlfriend.

Your Looking Glass

Before we go on, take a moment to reflect on what you've read so far about these three women's adult lives. Do you recognize yourself in their stories? Notice how you are feeling emotionally and physically. What thoughts are going through your head *right now*? Write them in your journal.

Mistrust/Abuse Quiz

Check the box (or boxes) that identify which coping style is still prominent in adulthood for Monica, Maggie, and Kelli.

	Overcompensation	Avoidance	Surrender
Monica	☐	☐	☐
Maggie	☐	☐	☐
Kelli	☐	☐	☐

Now pull out your journal and jot a few notes about Monica, Maggie, and Kelli. Where do you see their coping style(s) at work in their lives? Does codependency and/or shame play a role in their adult life? Recall that one coping style may be predominant, or they may use more than one.

(Answers are at the end of the chapter.)

Emotional Deprivation: Anita, Kathryn, and Vivienne

Women who had the life trap of emotional deprivation in childhood have this core belief: *no one is there for me.* As children, they were disappointed or let down by others who didn't understand them and/or who never kept promises or commitments to them; they were starved for love and nurturance. As adults, they still feel starved for love and nurturance. Narcissistic men are masters at making them feel loved and valuable. The woman often feels an extremely strong chemistry with the narcissist, which makes him impossible to ignore. When a woman with emotional deprivation meets this type of narcissistic man, she believes finally someone who understands her is there for her, and she'll never have to feel lonely again.

Anita

Anita's Childhood Coping Style: Overcompensation

Anita's Childhood: Anita's mother never knew or understood Anita. Her mother was narcissistic and her needs always trumped Anita's. Anita was frustrated and angry with her mother. They fought often.

Anita's Adulthood: Anita compensated for her feelings of never having her needs met by dating men whom she thought she could control. Nice men were attracted to her, but Anita was demanding of them. If they did not meet her demands, she was disappointed and left the relationship, or they tired of her demands and left her. She never gave these men a real chance. Her need for someone whom she felt really understood her made her ripe for a narcissistic relationship. The charming narcissist told her everything she wanted to hear. She immediately felt close to him, like he was the first person to really understand her. It was very seductive. But eventually his oh-so-charming ways turned into icy coldness. His prompt attentiveness to her turned to silence. She'd call him, but he was rarely available. When she finally reached him, he was aloof. The wonderful long telephone conversations she used to have with him where she felt so close now turned to brief uh-huhs and long pauses. When it was finally clear to her that he was no longer interested, she was devastated. It reinforced her belief that no one is there for her, that everyone disappoints her, and, therefore, she will likely always be alone.

Kathryn

Kathryn's Childhood Coping Style: Surrender

Kathryn's Childhood: Kathryn grew up in a rural area, the youngest of five. She was a bright child but received little guidance or nurturing. Her parents meant well, but they were poor and uneducated and did not understand the needs of a curious, intelligent child beyond food and clothing.

Kathryn's Adulthood: After high school, Kathryn was encouraged by one of her teachers to continue her education at the local junior college. Her teacher was able to get a small scholarship for her, but it only covered one year, and she could not afford to continue. Kathryn took a job in the closest town doing typing and filing, something she learned in high school. Her intent was to return to school at some point. She picked up skills quickly and was soon managing the office and making more money than her parents, whom she helped out financially. She was attracted to ambitious men with goals and a plan to attain them. Although she could not yet go after her own goals, it gave her a purpose to help them achieve theirs. But the men she was attracted to came with other baggage: they were only interested in themselves and their futures, not in her plans or goals. She would give a lot and receive little in return. She married one of them and never went back to college. She devoted herself to him. He did reach his goals—he convinced her that his goals were hers as well. According to him, he was doing everything for her. The man she married, who she thought would provide her with love and a purposeful life, turned out to be in it only for himself. She found herself lonely again.

Vivienne

Vivienne's Childhood Coping Styles: Surrender and avoidance

Vivienne's Childhood: Her mother was cold and detached, absorbed with the various men in her life. Try as she might to engage with her mother, she could not do it. Vivienne often felt alone.

Vivienne's Adulthood: Vivienne dated men who were unavailable because they were married or had a girlfriend; inappropriate because they were uneducated, unemployed, or both; or only after her money. She would pay for everything and rationalize that she could afford it and they could not. They were always so appreciative, and it made her feel special. Actually, she was buying love and ensuring that someone would be there for her, although she never saw it that way. She could never believe that someone loved her for herself. She certainly did not value herself. She continued to use food as a source of comfort to avoid her painful feelings. This caused her to be heavier than she liked, which fed into her belief that she was unlovable and not valuable. If a man was nice to her, she was immediately attracted to him. Her relationships always ended in disappointment. Yet she kept dating the same type of man: one who was unavailable and uninterested in her.

Your Looking Glass

Before we go on, take a moment to reflect on what you've read so far about these three women's adult lives. Do you recognize yourself in their stories? Notice how you are feeling emotionally and physically. What thoughts are going through your head *right now*? Write them in your journal.

Emotional Deprivation Quiz

Check the box (or boxes) that identify which coping style is still prominent in adulthood for Anita, Kathryn, and Vivienne.

	Overcompensation	Avoidance	Surrender
Anita	☐	☐	☐
Kathryn	☐	☐	☐
Vivienne	☐	☐	☐

Now pull out your journal and jot a few notes about Anita, Kathryn, and Vivienne. Where do you see their coping style(s) at work in their lives? Does codependency and/or shame play a role in their adult life? Recall that one coping style may be predominant, or they may use more than one.

(Answers are at the end of the chapter.)

Defectiveness/Shame: Pat, Kimberly, and Trisha

Women who had the life trap of defectiveness/shame in childhood have this core belief: *I'm not good enough to love.* They have a tremendous amount of shame because they believe they are intrinsically flawed in such a way that no one could possibly love them. They are attracted to the narcissistic man, who makes them feel worthy and valued—and then he changes. They stay in this unhealthy relationship with the narcissist and allow themselves to be criticized and mistreated, though, because they feel so badly about themselves.

Pat

Pat's Coping Style: Surrender

Pat's Childhood: Pat grew up as a tomboy in a home with a critical mother who was highly conscious of status and fashion. She was made to feel she was never good enough and that her mother was ashamed of her.

Pat's Adulthood: In an effort to please her mother, Pat was drawn to partners who were showy but actually not very interested in her. They eventually broke it off. She was fed up with these types of men. She wanted someone different. She met a man who was charming and kind to her. He liked to hold hands when they were outside and snuggle on the couch when they watched movies. These gestures made her feel cherished. He was quiet and reserved, definitely not the flashy type. She told herself she would never pick a flashy man again.

He did important work for children's charities for which he received many awards. He was self-righteous about this "important" work. And he often made her feel that things she was interested in were not as worthy as his work. At these times, she felt unimportant and not valued. No one would believe her if she told them that the quiet, reserved man who appeared to give so selflessly to children and others could be selfish and withholding when he was alone with her. Sometimes, in private, his quiet reserve could turn to icy coldness toward her. In time, she became more and more insecure and unhappy. She couldn't understand how she had ended up in another bad relationship; he'd seemed so different from the other men she dated.

Kimberly

Kimberly's Childhood Coping Style: Surrender

Kimberly's Childhood: Kimberly was only nine when a family friend who was renting a room in their house came into her bedroom one night and abused her. This continued for several years. Neither her parents nor her pediatrician ever recognized the clues that she tried desperately to give them.

Kimberly's Adulthood: Kimberly found every loser in a fifty-mile radius. She had such low self-esteem that she didn't think she had anything to offer anyone. Because of her shame and her belief that she was damaged, she allowed herself to be treated badly. Her last partner was the worst. He started out okay. He was interesting and intelligent, and they shared a love of music, but he was stubborn and critical. If she disagreed with him, he argued until he wore her down and she agreed with him. One evening they started arguing. It escalated, and he grabbed her by her hair and dragged her into the bedroom, where he threw her up against the wall. Another time, he had his fist in front of her face, threatening to hit her. She cringed, waiting for the blow, but he hit the wall instead of her face, breaking his hand. They went together to the emergency room, where she lied along with him and told the doctor a different story. As in her family, no one questioned her story.

Trisha

Trisha's Childhood Coping Style: Surrender

Trisha's Childhood: Trisha was a colicky baby and that is supposedly why her father left the family shortly after she was born. He, however, also abandoned his wife and several other older children, leaving them destitute. Everyone blamed Trisha for their poverty rather than the irresponsible father.

Trisha's Adulthood: One day while at the gym, Trisha met a guy who made snide remarks about everyone and everything, but they were funny, albeit opinionated, comments. He made her laugh in a naughty way. What she interpreted as confidence was actually bravado, overcompensation for his deep insecurities. His ardent pursuit of her made her feel valuable and special. He wanted to hear about all her thoughts, feelings, and opinions. She felt understood for the first time in her life. She had never had this connection with someone, so she ignored the red flags, such as the fact that he had a drinking problem and had been in multiple relationships but never married. He said he had just never met the right woman, and she bought it hook, line, and sinker. When he texted her throughout the day, she interpreted it as his passionate love for her rather than controlling behavior. Considering her core belief that she would never be good enough to love, he made her feel loved. But once he had her, all his bad behaviors came out.

He wanted to know her every move. If she didn't call him when she arrived somewhere, he accused her of meeting someone. He insisted on driving her to and from her job. She thought this was his way of showing his love for her, but, again, it actually was his controlling behavior. He would loiter by the receptionist, waiting for Trisha to finish work. Her boss told her she needed to ask him not to wait there every day. He also started drinking more. When he did, he became nasty in his accusations, or he demanded sex from her. If she refused his advances, he made her feel guilty. By then, she was powerless to leave him. Her desire to be loved trumped her reasoning.

Your Looking Glass

Before we go on, take a moment to reflect on what you've read so far about these three women's adult lives. Do you recognize yourself in their stories? Notice how you are feeling emotionally and physically. What thoughts are going through your head *right now*? Write them in your journal.

Defectiveness/Shame Quiz

Check the box (or boxes) that identify which coping style is still prominent in adulthood for Pat, Kimberly, and Trisha.

	Overcompensation	Avoidance	Surrender
Pat	☐	☐	☐
Kimberly	☐	☐	☐
Trisha	☐	☐	☐

Now pull out your journal and jot a few notes about Pat, Kimberly, and Trisha. Where do you see their coping style(s) at work in their lives? Does codependency and/or shame play a role in their adult life? Recall that one coping style may be predominant, or they may use more than one.

(Answers are at the end of the chapter.)

Subjugation: Alice, Petra, and Marty

Women who had the life trap of subjugation in childhood have this core belief: *if I don't meet others' needs, they won't care about me.* As adults, these women are people pleasers. They believe they have no choice but to go along with whatever someone wants and never voice their opinion, wants, or needs for fear of the other person becoming mad, or worse, of losing the other person's affection. They are attracted to narcissistic men, who initially make them feel loved and cared for, but when the narcissist changes, these women are the perfect partner for a man who is selfish, demanding, and controlling.

Alice

Alice's Childhood Coping Style: Surrender

Alice's Childhood: Alice was a shy, reserved, soft-spoken little girl. Her mother was domineering and controlling.

Alice's Adulthood: Alice continued the pattern of not having her needs met when she made dating choices. When she was in a relationship, she put her partner's needs and desires ahead of her own for fear of losing his love. She ended up with men who were selfish and controlling. For example, when they went out, her boyfriend would monopolize the dinner conversation with stories of his day but never ask about how her day had gone. Alice would listen attentively and never talk about herself. One Valentine's Day, Alice, a foodie who liked to go to the newest and trendiest restaurants, assumed her boyfriend would take her to a certain restaurant she had told him she was interested in trying. She was disappointed when he took her instead to his favorite steak house, but she never expressed her disappointment. She put up with the narcissist's bad behaviors because it seemed so familiar to respond to his demands.

She rarely allowed herself to feel anger or resentment, but when she occasionally let her frustration boil over, her partner withdrew his affection, just as her mother had done. One time when they planned to go to a movie, they couldn't agree on what to see. He insisted on his choice. For once, Alice took the risk and refused to go with him. Alice could feel he was furious, but he didn't say anything and just left. Alice waited up for him, but he didn't come home until very late and then just went to bed without saying anything. Alice was so nervous that he'd break up with her that she apologized the next day. Alice put up with a lot of her partner's demanding and controlling behaviors. Eventually, he ended the relationship, but soon she was in another one with just the same type of man.

Petra

Petra's Childhood Coping Styles: Surrender and overcompensation

Petra's Childhood: Petra was raised in a strict religious family. She was indoctrinated to believe that always putting others first was of value and that asserting her own desires, wants, and needs was selfish.

Petra's Adulthood: Petra moved to a large city when she was offered a job teaching art in a grade school. Her parents were unhappy about this, because it was not a religious school. Since she had never learned to stand up for herself, men could easily take advantage of her and control her. One boyfriend often borrowed money from her and never paid her back. He always promised to but then found some excuse. Another one would ask her to help straighten up his apartment when she was over, then he'd leave to run a "quick errand" and not return for a couple hours, leaving her to clean his whole apartment. Another partner, a fellow teacher, was always behind in his classroom paperwork because he chose to play video games instead. Alice always came to his rescue by writing his lesson plans and grading his papers. He watched TV or played a video game while she did his work. She felt she was being selfish if she asked for anything. She always tried to give these men the benefit of the doubt or to rationalize how their interests were more important than hers. She was miserable at times but would not admit it to herself. Maybe this was God's plan and there was something she was to learn—something such as humility?

Marty

Marty's Childhood Coping Styles: Surrender and avoidance

Marty's Childhood: Her father was a highly controlling military man. It was his way or the highway.

Marty's Adulthood: Marty picked men who seemed caring yet in control and commanding, like her father. They were also demanding and domineering. If she didn't meet their expectations or needs, they became irritable. Marty was uncomfortable when they got mad, fearing she had made a mistake and would be in trouble. Because she hated feeling that way, Marty always obliged them to avoid conflict and be like the good girl she had been growing up. She wanted more than anything to keep the peace and be a good girlfriend or wife.

The man she married did not like to socialize. He was cynical and misanthropic. He believed he was superior to the people he met. Marty enjoyed people and wanted to entertain, but he made it uncomfortable for guests by challenging them on things they brought up or by questioning them on things he knew very few people would know the answer to. Marty stopped entertaining because it was not worth it. Her husband also liked to plan extensive trips. Marty would have preferred staying at a nice resort, but her husband insisted they travel off road and camp. Marty felt she had no choice but to accommodate her husband, so she soldiered on as the good-girl-now-wife to her husband's demands. She felt the same sense of powerlessness she had as a child.

Your Looking Glass

Before we go on, take a moment to reflect on what you've read so far about these three women. Do you recognize yourself in their stories? Notice how you are feeling emotionally and physically. What thoughts are going through your head *right now*? Write them in your journal.

Subjugation Quiz

Check the box (or boxes) that identify which coping style is still prominent in adulthood for Alice, Petra, and Marty.

	Overcompensation	Avoidance	Surrender
Alice	☐	☐	☐
Petra	☐	☐	☐
Marty	☐	☐	☐

Now pull out your journal and jot a few notes about Alice, Petra, and Marty. Where do you see their coping style(s) at work in their lives? Does codependency and/or shame play a role in their adult life? Recall that one coping style may be predominant, or they may use more than one.

(Answers are at the end of the chapter.)

Self-Sacrifice: Dianne, Marlene, and Lily

Women with this life trap in childhood have the following core belief: *I need to help or fix others, and I choose to do so.* Now as adult women, they are attracted to narcissistic men who they perceive need them. Because women with this life trap are highly empathic, they make excuses for their partners' bad behaviors and try to help them. They never give up on their partners.

Dianne

Dianne's Childhood Coping Style: Surrender

Dianne's Childhood: Dianne was eleven when her mother was diagnosed with multiple sclerosis. Dianne had two younger siblings. As her mother's condition grew worse, Dianne pitched in to help more.

Dianne's Adulthood: As an adult, Dianne was always extremely sensitive to the suffering of people and animals. She could not stand to see anyone's pain, emotional or physical. She was the type of person others confided in or came to for help. She always made herself available to others. When she made dating choices, she was attracted to men who needed her help. They were selfish men, absorbed in their own lives. Often they were addicted to drugs or alcohol, came from dysfunctional families, or had financial difficulties. She tried tirelessly to help them and, in doing so, gave much more than she received. She would not give up on a partner. Every boyfriend she had took advantage of her selflessness, some more than others. One boyfriend took her credit card and ran up $2,500 in charges. Dianne was hurt and angry but accepted his tearful apology and didn't break up with him. She rationalized his behavior as being due to his dysfunctional childhood. She felt sorry for him and didn't insist that he pay her back. Another time, he pawned her laptop for drug money. Again, she did nothing. She tried to help him set up a budget and find extra work, and provided him with a stable home. She believed that he just needed to be shown that someone would always be there for him. But no matter how much she did for him, he didn't change. He continued to do whatever he wanted and to take advantage of her kindness. She continued to love him and believe she could help him. She stopped complaining about him to her friends. She was ashamed she was still with him, but she couldn't help herself.

Marlene

Marlene's Childhood Coping Style: Surrender

Marlene's Childhood: Marlene's father died of a sudden heart attack when he was in his early forties. Her mother became sad and depressed.

Marlene hated to see her mother unhappy. She wanted more than anything to take away her mother's pain.

Marlene's Adulthood: As an adult, Marlene picked partners who were controlling and manipulating. If her rights, needs, or desires were different from theirs, they were easily injured. Somehow they turned things around and made her the selfish one. One in particular made her feel guilty by telling her how much he did for her and that he was only asking for small things in return. One time he wanted to go with his guy friends to Las Vegas. She was angry because that was supposed to be a weekend for them. He hung his head and sulked. He told her about all the times he had taken her to dinners and on vacations. But the dinners were always at new restaurants he wanted to try, and the vacations were work-related ones. He invited her to come with him because he wanted someone to hang out with between work sessions or to do things he liked, such as golfing. He had a way of making her believe the sky was green and the grass was blue, so before she knew it, Marlene felt guilty about not letting him go to Vegas and she tried harder to win his approval and make him happy. Occasionally, she felt some resentment, but she immediately felt guilty for having these feelings and buried them. She consoled herself, saying that she was fine and that he needed "it," whatever the "it" was, more than she did.

Lily

Lily's Childhood Coping Style: Surrender

Lily's Childhood: She had a younger brother with dwarfism whom she tried to protect. Lily did not want to add to her family's burden, so she took on more and more responsibility.

Lily's Adulthood: As an adult, Lily picked partners who were irresponsible and unreliable. This left her to be the reliable one who took care of things. Although she felt needed and useful, she never got her needs met.

Still she could not help but take care of others. Her partners made Lily feel guilty and called her selfish when she asked to do something her way. She felt guilty whenever she put herself first, asserted herself, or asked for her needs to be met. The man she married was fun and funny and never seemed to get angry or upset, but he forgot to mention before they married that he had $55,000 in credit card debt. She found out when they were going to buy a house together. She assumed his debt, rationalizing that this is what married couples do. He insisted on paying all the bills and handling the money, saying he had learned his lesson and wanted to show her how responsible he could be. She adhered to a strict budget, denying herself any small luxury in order to pay off "their" debt. When she asked to look at their bank or credit card statements, he would tell her there was nothing to see. If she continued to ask, he played the victim card, saying she didn't trust him and that he was trying his best. She would feel sorry for him and back off. In time, she found out he was gambling online and increasing their debt, not decreasing it.

Your Looking Glass

Before we go on, take a moment to reflect on what you've read so far about these three women. Do you recognize yourself in their stories? Notice how you are feeling emotionally and physically. What thoughts are going through your head *right now*? Write them in your journal.

Self-Sacrifice Quiz

Check the box (or boxes) that identify which coping style is still prominent in adulthood for Dianne, Marlene, and Lily.

	Overcompensation	Avoidance	Surrender
Dianne	☐	☐	☐
Marlene	☐	☐	☐
Lily	☐	☐	☐

Now pull out your journal and jot a few notes about Dianne, Marlene, and Lily. Where do you see their coping style(s) at work in their lives? Does codependency and/or shame play a role in their adult life? Recall that one coping style may be predominant, or they may use more than one.

(Answers are at the end of the chapter.)

Unrelenting Standards: Jennifer, Chelsea, and Elspeth

Women who had the life trap of unrelenting standards in childhood have this core belief: *whatever I do, it'll never be good enough*. In adulthood, they are attracted to narcissistic partners who make them feel they are special and that everything they do is perfect and wonderful. But when the narcissist shows his true colors and becomes critical, these women strive to meet all his ridiculous, unrealistic demands in an effort to regain the man who praised them in the beginning. Trying to meet his incessant, unreasonable demands keeps them a prisoner in the narcissist's world.

Jennifer

Jennifer's Childhood Coping Style: Surrender

Jennifer's Childhood: She grew up in a family where it was not okay to make a mistake. She loved her father dearly, but she only got his love and attention when she succeeded. If she fell short in any way, he shamed her by expressing his deep disappointment.

Jennifer's Adulthood: As an adult, Jennifer was driven to succeed. It was not good enough to be average. She wanted to be the best. At work, she imposed rigid goals for herself. She came in early and stayed later than anyone else. She took work home on the weekends or came in to the office to work. In her dating life, she was attracted to men who were also ambitious and driven, but as critical narcissists, they always made her feel that she was not quite good enough. She would try harder to meet their needs, to measure up to their expectations, but it was an uphill climb. The more she tried to attain perfection, the more it eluded her. Her health suffered, since she wasn't taking care of herself—eating on the run and not getting regular exercise or sleep. She dated narcissist after narcissist, and with each man, she tried to live up to his expectations, but he would always let her know how she fell short by giving her a disapproving look, pouting, or grumbling some criticism about her.

With one guy in particular, she walked on eggshells at his home, anticipating that she'd make a mistake. He had very specific ways of doing things and insisted that she comply. They ranged from things like how she hung up her clothes, which hangers she used, and which way they faced, to how she placed the kitchen water faucet when she turned it off. He even complained that she breathed too loudly when he talked to her on the phone—and on and on. He would get exasperated when he had to remind her how something should be done. How many times did he have to tell or show her? One time he actually told her that she just couldn't be trained. She couldn't understand how, even when she mastered the list of things he wanted her to do correctly, new things kept being added to the list. She never did anything well enough, but she kept trying.

Chelsea

Chelsea's Childhood Coping Style: Surrender

Chelsea's Childhood: Her parents valued status and wealth. Chelsea adopted their values and spent all her time striving to meet their standards and thus win their love and approval. Even with all the material things she acquired, she never felt like it was enough. She thought she would feel good about herself when she surrounded herself with status and wealth, but she still felt empty and unhappy.

Chelsea's Adulthood: Chelsea was attracted to men who were at the top of their game in terms of status and wealth. Because she was only interested in their stats, she didn't pay attention to their obvious faults, such as enormous egos and superior airs. All she could see was how her partner fit into the scenario of her future, being the wife of Mr. X, the CEO, president, or senator. She paid a high price emotionally for the man she eventually married.

Although he was the CEO of a major financial institution and had the six-figure income to prove it, he was self-absorbed and emotionally unavailable. He, too, was focused on achieving status and wealth to compensate for his feelings of inadequacy. He couldn't love her because he had no idea what a real loving relationship looked like. After any important fund-raiser, they'd come home and he would immediately go into his office and check e-mails, leaving Chelsea alone. If she went to him, he'd tell her to go to bed and that he'd be up in a short while. Most nights she went to bed alone. Chelsea had everything she wanted in terms of material things, but she felt empty inside, as if something was missing. She never felt satisfied, and she certainly was not happy.

Elspeth

Elspeth's Childhood Coping Styles: Surrender and overcompensation

Elspeth's Childhood: Her parents had high standards that they expected their children to adhere to. Elspeth became obsessed with getting all the details perfect and berated herself mercilessly if she did not.

Elspeth's Adulthood: As an adult, Elspeth dated men who were critical, controlling, and rigid. Of course, they never started out this way. Like all narcissists, they started out adoring and caring. When their demands came out, she paid attention to every detail, because Elspeth was hardwired to be perfect, and she had a competitive nature. Whatever it took, she would meet her partner's demands. If he criticized her hair or makeup, she was on it, immediately making appointments with makeup artists and stylists to fit his view of an ideal woman. Elspeth was the type to obsessively count calories to maintain her perfect figure. She made detailed workout routines that she followed religiously. If she had to miss a workout, she became frustrated with herself. She needed everything to be planned and orderly.

Though Elspeth bent over backward to meet all his demands, his one small criticism always told her she never quite got it right. She joined him for "fun" weekend runs, but he always ran to beat her, staying a stride ahead of her at all times. Try as she might, she could never catch up. She wouldn't admit it to herself, but she wasn't enjoying any aspect of her relationship. She was always in fear of doing something wrong, and this made her edgy and irritable at times. The finish line kept moving farther and farther away. Elspeth never reached a goal because she knew she could do it even better. This belief kept her in prison with a controlling, critical narcissist.

Your Looking Glass

Before we go on, take a moment to reflect on what you've read so far about these three women. Do you recognize yourself in their stories? Notice how you are feeling emotionally and physically. What thoughts are going through your head *right now*? Write them in your journal.

Unrelenting Standards Quiz

Check the box (or boxes) that identify which coping style is still prominent in adulthood for Jennifer, Chelsea, and Elspeth.

	Overcompensation	Avoidance	Surrender
Jennifer	☐	☐	☐
Chelsea	☐	☐	☐
Elspeth	☐	☐	☐

Now pull out your journal and jot a few notes about Jennifer, Chelsea, and Elspeth. Where do you see their coping style(s) at work in their lives? Does codependency and/or shame play a role in their adult life? Recall that one coping style may be predominant, or they may use more than one.

(Answers are at the end of the chapter.)

Exercise 8: *Which Life Traps Are Still at Play Within You?*

In your journal, write a narrative of your adulthood, including your romantic relationships. Use the questions below to help you write this narrative:

1. How did you meet? Were there any red flags you missed? For example, did he only talk about himself and never ask about you, or he was very quiet but blew up at the parking attendant?

2. What adjectives would you use to describe each man with whom you were in a relationship (for example, cold, detached, Machiavellian, duplicitous, trying, and so on)?

3. Which life trap(s) do you have? Which life trap predominates for you now? Is this life trap different than your childhood life trap?

4. Did shame play a role in your adult intimate relationships? In what way?

5. Do you think you are codependent in your adult intimate relationships? If yes, write examples of the behaviors you identify as codependent.

6. Think of how you manage your painful feelings. Do you use one of the coping styles of overcompensation, avoidance, or surrender? Do you use more than one coping style? Is one more prominent than others?

Exercise 9: *Key Words*

If you'd rather not write out a narrative, jot down some key words in your journal that describe your adult life and your situation—for example, lonely, unhappy, miserable, fearful, and so on.

Exercise 10: *Complete the Sentence*

If you'd rather, write the phrases below in your journal and then complete each sentence to reflect what you wish your partners were like.

- I want my partner to…

    OR

- "[Partner's name], what I really want from you is…"

Then ask yourself if there is a deeper layer to your answer. For example, you may have said that you wanted your partner to stop *criticizing* you but the deeper layer is that you wanted him to *love you unconditionally*, just for yourself. You wanted to feel special.

Putting It All Together

In this chapter, we focused on how childhood life traps are manifested in adulthood and impact your dating choices. You also saw how the coping styles of overcompensation, avoidance, and surrender might change from childhood to adulthood. You had the opportunity to consider if shame, vulnerability, or codependence had a role in your dating choices or relationships. In the next chapter, you will learn how to change your life traps by changing your core beliefs.

Quiz Answers

Abandonment: Clare, Kirsten, and Lynette

Clare: overcompensation (is clingy) and avoidance (accepts her husband's cheating behavior to avoid conflict)

Kirsten: avoidance (not thinking about it, denies how bad it is) and surrender (tries to have another child to save the marriage and to not be alone)

Lynette: avoidance (ignores red flags) and surrender (accepts it's her fault, begs for forgiveness, picks unhealthy men, takes the abuse)

Mistrust/Abuse: Monica, Maggie, and Kelli

Monica: avoidance (stops dating to avoid pain)

Maggie: overcompensation (people pleaser, goes along with husband's demands)

Kelli: overcompensation (attracted to powerful men) and surrender (takes abuse)

Emotional Deprivation: Anita, Kathryn, and Vivienne

Anita: overcompensation (dating men she thinks she can control and being demanding of others)

Kathryn: overcompensation (attracted to ambitious men) and surrender (does not ask for her emotional needs to be met)

Vivienne: overcompensation (pays for everything), avoidance (uses food for comfort), and surrender (picks emotionally unavailable men)

Defectiveness: Pat, Kimberly, and Trisha

Pat: overcompensation (dates showy men) and surrender (selects critical men and is self-deprecating)

Kimberly: surrender (picks abusive men)

Trisha: avoidance (ignores partner's red flags)

Subjugation: Alice, Petra, and Marty

Alice: avoidance (doesn't voice her opinions in order to avoid conflict, people pleaser)

Petra: overcompensation (does for others in order to get love) and surrender (puts others' needs ahead of her own)

Marty: surrender (picks men like her father)

Self-Sacrifice: Dianne, Marlene, and Lily

Dianne: surrender (gives to others, asks little in return)

Marlene: avoidance (avoids thinking about how bad the relationship is) and surrender (gives to others, asks little in return)

Lily: surrender (gives to others, asks little in return)

Unrelenting Standards: Jennifer, Chelsea, and Elspeth

Jennifer: avoidance (walks on eggshells to avoid being judged or making a mistake) and surrender (accepts what she does is never good enough, picks ambitious men)

Chelsea: surrender (accepts what she does is never good enough, dates wealthy men for status)

Elspeth: avoidance (does not admit to herself how unhappy she is) and surrender (accepts what she does is never good enough)

CHAPTER 6

Learn to Change Your Life Traps

Now you are aware of your own coping styles and have a much greater awareness of how your life traps have influenced your dating choices. You know more than when you started, but you're still fragile, like a fledgling that's not yet strong enough to fly freely and confidently. Too often women want to hurry the process. They think because they now have insight into their life traps and coping styles that they're ready to date again. But insight is only the beginning of change. If you stop at insight without learning important skills, the weight of your life traps will cause you to fall back into another bad relationship with a narcissistic man. Trust me, you need to strengthen your muscles and learn some maneuvers before you take off. I want you to succeed and soar into romantic bliss, so let's take it slow.

As you contemplate your move away from your endless cycle of narcissistic relationships, you may find it helpful to think of the process as being similar to recovery from an addiction. In the beginning, addicts are fragile and need a lot of support in the form of groups, friends, family, and a sponsor. Even with all of their new awareness and support, they can easily relapse until they learn how to maintain their abstinence. To do this, they have to learn how to think and behave differently. This is a slow, deliberate process. Over time, they learn a new way to live without their addiction. The result is a much happier and more satisfying life. As with addiction, you need to integrate the building blocks needed to change your pattern of dating narcissistic men, and, more important, learn how to maintain that change.

It's critical, however, to know that *change is possible*. I have seen many women heal, change, and grow. Remember Jessica, the doctor who dated

Ethan and Todd and had to support her dependent parents? Just this week, she came to her appointment and showed me her beautiful engagement ring. She finally found a "good one" who really loves her, and I am fully confident that you will, too. Let's start building your skills to help you soar free.

Essential Elements

This chapter focuses on the first building blocks needed to change your life traps. You will learn the steps to behavioral change and how to maintain that change. You will also learn how to develop and integrate the skills of mindful breathing, mindfulness meditation, and realistic thinking into your life. Like strengthening your muscles, these skills will become stronger with practice.

How Behavioral Change Takes Place

Behavioral change begins when you believe three things: (1) a new behavior is necessary, (2) it's possible to change your old behavior, and (3) you will be successful in your attempts to change. When you really believe changing a particular behavior is necessary, you will be motivated to change. Maybe you have high blood pressure, are a borderline diabetic, or are just sick of the yo-yo pattern of gaining and losing that five, ten, twenty, or more pounds. Only when you really believe that your health is more important than the pizza or ice cream you indulge in—sort of a cost-benefit analysis—will you be motivated to change your behavior and adopt a healthier lifestyle. But you also have to believe that it's possible to achieve this change, or you won't even bother to try. Too often we want to change, but we don't really believe it's possible because we have tried so many times before and failed. Over time, this saps our motivation to try yet again. But when you understand the steps to behavioral change, you can make a plan that really works. What I am going to teach you works for all behavioral change, including no longer repeating unhealthy narcissistic relationships. I know this plan will work for you as it has for countless other women. The plan is based on James Prochaska and colleagues' six stages of behavioral change:[16]

Stage 1: Precontemplation

Stage 2: Contemplation

Stage 3: Preparation/determination

Stage 4: Activation

Stage 5: Maintenance

Stage 6: Relapse

Let's look at how you would change a behavior associated with the life trap of abandonment. Say you found out your boyfriend or partner had been cheating, and he'd lied to you about it for months. You went through the back-and-forth, the trying to believe him when he begged forgiveness and said it was a stupid mistake, and because you wanted to believe him, you did. But months later, it happened again. Now you are done. You ended the relationship, and it still hurts horribly, but you know you had to let the relationship—and him—go. Doing this was so difficult for you because ending relationships stirs up all your abandonment fears. You can't help but wonder, *Did I cause him to cheat by being too clingy?* Now you are alone, maybe forever, and you feel scared and anxious. But you continually look at social media to find out what he's doing and what his life is like. You see pictures of him enjoying his life and you get so upset, but you can't stop yourself. You're embarrassed by how obsessed you are. Your therapist has told you to stop as have all your friends. Of course, it's easier said than done. So how are you going to do it? This is exactly what Christy went through. I taught her the six stages of change, and she gave it a try. The italicized comments below are Christy's and the "Ask yourself" question at the end is for you. Here's what happened for Christy.

Stage 1. Precontemplation

You deny having a significant problem and/or minimize it.

Example: Christy had thoughts like these: *I know I should probably cut off ties. I should stop "stalking" him on social media, and I should block his phone number. Everyone says I should stop checking out his life on social media, but what's the real harm? He doesn't know I am looking at him. It helps me to see what he's doing.*

Ask yourself: Do I have a problem with letting go?

Stage 2. Contemplation

You give a little more thought to the problem, considering the costs versus the benefits and how to go about making the change.

Example: Christy thought, *If I stop looking at pictures of his life on social media, maybe I can begin to let go. But then I won't see what he's doing! The truth is, though, when I see him with friends having a good time, or worse with a girl in the picture, I feel terrible about myself.*

Ask yourself: What are the pros and cons of continuing to check up on him?

Stage 3. Preparation/Determination

Once you accept your cost-benefit analysis that you need to stop "stalking" him on social media and that the benefit is worth it—being free of the pain—you focus more specifically on how you will change—you determine your goal—and then set up a time line for achieving that goal. Having a specific rather than general goal is key. Also, sharing your plan with others will help you keep your resolve. You might write a contract with yourself outlining what you will do and the rationale for doing it.

Example: Christy thought, *My plan will start immediately. I will put up a sticky note that says "No!" on my computer screen and bathroom mirror to remind me not to go online to check up on him. I will write a narrative of all the terrible things he did to me and look at it every time I feel a longing for him. When I think of him, I will pull my awareness back to me and think about my goals for the future. I will go for a walk when I have the urge to check him out. I will ask my friends to help me by being available if I need to talk. I will keep track of my progress as I go along. Focusing on my future is my ultimate goal, not watching his life!*

Ask yourself: What *specific* things can I do to help myself change?

Stage 4. Activation

Follow the course you set in place to make the change.

Example: Christy thought, *I will put up the sticky notes, walk out the door any time I have the urge to check him out, use my friends for support, and think about my goals every time I think of him. I will journal about all of this and give myself lovely rewards for focusing on my life and not his.*

Ask yourself: If I keep track of my progress, will it help me to stay on course and be motivated?

Stage 5. Maintenance

Identify obstacles that may derail your success, make a plan to manage them, and stay vigilant.

Example: Christy thought, *On weekends, I may feel lonely and sad. I may slip one weekend or have a mini-breakdown, really tanking myself with horrible thoughts about what a loser I am, how I'll never find someone, and how time is going by. I have identified that weekends are clearly an obstacle. So, first, I'll predict that weekends are an obstacle, and second, I'll make a plan for them. I'll be sure to make weekend plans with friends by Wednesday, and I will make plans for the evenings when I feel especially lonely.*

Your plans may include activities with friends, but also things to improve your life such as yoga, running, lectures, gardening, or whatever. Remind yourself how much better you feel when you don't moon over him and check him out online. Remind yourself of your goal and embrace your new healthy lifestyle.

Ask yourself: How do I feel about the changes I am making? How confident am I that I can maintain them?

Stage 6. Relapse

Relapse is a return to an earlier stage of change for a significant period of time.

Example: Christy remembered, *I not only looked at him on Facebook, but I sent him a private message saying, "I like your vacation pictures." He never responded, and now I feel terrible about myself. Yet I continued to look at him frequently on social media, checking for a return message from him.*

Relapse can go on for a long while. When this occurs, you lose your resolve and motivation to continue to change. In time, you return to an earlier stage of change, perhaps contemplation, remembering why it is important to change.

You may also experience a *slip*, a simple departure from your action plan. For example, maybe you looked at him on social media one time, you recognized this was not following your action plan, and the next day you returned to your regular plan of taking care of yourself by focusing on *you*, not him. Because slips can precede relapses, it is important to correct them before they result in a full-blown relapse.

Ask yourself: Is this a slip or a relapse? If a relapse, what were the conditions that created it?

As we all go through these stages of change, relapse is obviously the one that tanks our motivation. But it's important to understand and accept that it is normal to relapse. We may not like it, but it can happen. Relapse can occur when we have a series of slips, when other things take precedence in our life and we stop following our plan of change, or when we face an unexpected obstacle. The key is not to get so frustrated that you quit. Too many people want to quit after multiple relapses. They feel that they will never be successful, that nothing works. I have heard women say, "I have tried everything and nothing works." It's true they have tried everything, but they never learned how to maintain change, and they gave up after they relapsed. False starts, achievements, slips, and relapses are normal in the course of changing behavior. I tell the women I work with that behavioral change is a process: it's two steps forward, one step back. Sometimes I picture it like a spiral slope circling back around itself on the way up. The point is, it is still going in the right direction—*you* are going in the right direction—toward change. It's a process.

By taking the time to identify the circumstances that led to the relapse, you can learn how to avoid or handle them next time. And the research is clear. The more attempts you make, the more likely you will eventually experience successful long-term maintenance. So instead of being fearful that you will relapse, accept it as a normal part of behavioral change. Instead of becoming discouraged, think of it as an opportunity to learn what else you will need to change in order to be successful. In fact, you can even think of a relapse as a sign that you are doing something right. If you weren't making an effort to change, if you weren't even trying, you wouldn't have a relapse—you'd be swallowed up by the destructive behavior all the time. So, whether you have a slip or a relapse, don't quit. Just figure out what went wrong and correct it so it doesn't happen again.

Your Looking Glass

Now that you have read this section, I know you *want* to change and you know you *need* to change. How confident are you that you can stop repeating narcissistic relationships? Take a minute to reflect on your concerns about your ability to change. Write them in your journal and explore why you feel this way. Is it because you have failed in the past? Is it because you don't think you are smart enough to change? How are these thoughts related to your life traps? Your core beliefs? It's normal to feel ambivalence about change.

Exercise 11: *Changing a Behavior*

Think of a behavior associated with a life trap that you want to change. In your journal, list the six stages of change. Then, using those six stages, write down your plan for changing your life trap. Be sure to include specific goals, a detailed action plan, specific obstacles you might face, and a plan for how to manage them. Take your time with this. You're taking a big step here, and you need to honor yourself for having the courage to do this.

Now that you have identified the life trap you need to change and have written out your six stages to change, here are some skills to help you achieve the change you desire.

Skills to Change Your Life Traps

Mindful breathing, mindfulness meditation, and realistic thinking are truly the building blocks of change. To me, they are the foundation for *any* change, and I use them routinely in my practice. They are incredibly effective in helping to change unhealthy ways of thinking and responding. And I use them myself, too, every day. But as with any skill, to learn to use them well takes practice, practice, practice—and commitment. They'll feel a bit awkward at first. It's sort of like when you first learned to ride your bike without training wheels. For a long time, you felt like you'd never get the hang of it, but you persevered because you wanted it. After a while, you could ride without even thinking about it. The skills of mindful breathing, mindfulness meditation, and realistic thinking will help you manage your core beliefs, which have become automatic and habitual. They will help you increase your awareness, assess and evaluate your negative patterns of thinking and feeling, and learn how to respond differently, all of which are necessary to change your life traps.

Mindful Breathing

The first skill, mindful breathing, has wonderful benefits to well-being. It sounds simple, yet it is amazing how many people don't practice it correctly. (Mindful breathing is not only an important skill on its own but also provides a foundation for the practice of mindfulness meditation, which is the next skill you will learn to help change your life traps.) Mindful breathing is also called deep breathing, abdominal breathing, or diaphragmatic breathing. Healthy adults breathe automatically about twelve to twenty breaths per minute. You might be surprised to know you are likely doing it incorrectly. To prove it, go right now and stand in front of a mirror. Watch yourself breathe. You will no doubt think, *Hey, what's the big deal?* But take a closer look at yourself as you breathe in. You will probably notice your shoulders and/or your chest rise and fall with each breath. If you can't see it, just put one hand on your chest and your other hand on your tummy at your navel. What do you see? Do you see and feel your chest hand move up and down and your tummy hand remaining still? If you do, then you are breathing incorrectly. Sure, you are getting oxygen in your lungs, but you are not getting it deep into the lower lobes of your lungs. Your way of breathing is called "thoracic breathing," or chest breathing. The proper way to breathe is to inhale deeply. When you breathe this way, you'll see your tummy hand extend and recede with every breath, your chest hand remain still, and your shoulders remain still as well. At one time in your life, you actually did breathe correctly. Watch a baby breathing while asleep. You will see the baby's tummy moving up and down. Somehow as we grew up, we lost this ability to breathe correctly.

Although it seems natural, chest breathing is not, and it can actually increase tension and anxiety. With chest breathing, your breaths are shallow and are not fully oxygenating the lower lobes of your lungs, so you are not getting as much oxygen as you are designed to take in. This can lead to feeling shortness of breath.

If you are someone prone to anxiety or if you are just experiencing stress in your life, you may notice that you often feel tightness, like a steel band, across your chest. This is because you are holding tension in your shoulders. This tension causes you to tighten and hunch your shoulders without you even realizing you're doing it. This contributes to chest breathing and subsequently not getting enough oxygen deep into the lower lobes of your lungs. When people have anxiety attacks, they often describe their shortness of breath and what feels like a steel band around their chest.

Remember the stress response—fight, flight, or freeze? Daily hassles continually activate our body's stress response, causing us to stay in this heightened level of arousal. This takes a toll on our body's immune system and can contribute to all sorts of health problems, such as high blood pressure, increased anxiety and depression, heart disease, and decreased immune functioning, which makes us more susceptible to colds and other infections. Deep breathing stops the stress response by allowing for full oxygen exchange. It slows down the heartbeat and can lower or stabilize blood pressure. Mindful breathing can help you change your life trap because it helps you remain relaxed. When Christy was home alone and becoming scared and anxious, she would take a few minutes to sit quietly and focus on her breathing. She found her anxiety would pass and, along with it, her desire to check social media. Instead, she could focus on her life and do something good for herself, like make a nice dinner or watch a movie. Because it's important in so many ways, let's practice mindful breathing.

Exercise 12: *Mindful Breathing*

Stand in front of a mirror. Place one hand on your tummy and one on your chest. See if you can breathe through your lower tummy. Try it for one minute. Or you can lie flat and try it. Sometimes that makes it easier to feel.

You want to make this your normal way of breathing. (I actually can't breathe any other way now that I've learned it.) Try saying a quieting word like *calm* or *relax* to yourself as you breathe, as you inhale and exhale. Sometimes I like to envision color. I'll see the air as gold or white filling my lungs and body as I inhale, and pink or lavender as I exhale. Choose whichever colors you like.

Mindful breathing is a skill. You can use it to relax and give respite to your body and mind. I recommend you start by practicing mindful breathing for one minute a day and work up to ten minutes a day. This is a skill that not only relaxes you but also recharges you. It slows down your day and brings you into the present. Practice mindful breathing at least once a day or as many times as you like to relax and become refreshed, or just to center yourself during a particularly stressful day. Next, you will learn mindfulness meditation. To begin, let me give you a little background on mindfulness and mindfulness meditation.

Mindfulness Meditation

The practice of mindfulness, derived from Buddhism, is a way to gain insight and awareness into your thoughts, actions, and patterns of thinking and responding. These insights will help you change negative core beliefs and the unhealthy, habitual pattern of repeating narcissistic relationships.

Mindfulness is a form of meditation. I know you may be thinking, *Ugh, don't tell me I have to meditate. Yawn.* Yes, you do, because this is a really important and valuable skill. I promise. It is called "mindfulness" because as you meditate, you pay attention to—you are "mindful" of—your thoughts and bodily sensations. You do so without expectation or judgments, such as *I shouldn't think this way* or *I'm a terrible person. No wonder he doesn't like me* or *I'll never be able to do this.* Instead, you simply observe your thoughts. It is like watching a movie screen with your thoughts drifting across it. All you have to do is watch them go by. Don't hold on to them or judge them. Just let them be.

So what does this mean? Instead of avoiding our negative core beliefs, we acknowledge them, without judgment. This frees us to heal and relax. If you want to know more about mindfulness, and I encourage that, I suggest you start with the book *A Mindfulness-Based Stress Reduction Workbook* by Bob Stahl and Elisha Goldstein.[17] This book will guide you through a program of mindfulness-based stress reduction (MBSR) that was originally developed at the University of Massachusetts Medical School. Mindfulness meditation has incredible health and wellness benefits:

- strengthening of your immune system

- increase in feelings of well-being and happiness

- decrease in stress response so you disengage faster from emotionally upsetting situations

- acceleration of the speed by which you process information, thus improving concentration and attention

- decrease in anxiety, including racing thoughts or rumination (thoughts you can't get out of your head)

As you can see, the practice of mindfulness meditation can help you address and change the negative core beliefs associated with your life trap. Specifically, it helps you learn to be less judgmental of yourself, to increase self-acceptance, and to stop being a prisoner of your negative thoughts and core beliefs. I think of mindfulness meditation as magic. Once you learn it, I guarantee you will, too.

Exercise 13: *Formal Mindfulness Meditation*

This mindfulness meditation is best if done daily. If you have never meditated before, I suggest starting with one minute of meditation and eventually working up to three minutes or more. I usually set a timer on my cell phone, but an egg timer will work as well.

1. Assume any position in which you feel comfortable—sit, stand, or lie down. There is no prescribed position. You can have your eyes open or shut, whichever you prefer. I think it's easier with your eyes closed, but that's me.

2. Use your mindful breathing skill to inhale deeply and exhale, breathing through your abdomen in a relaxed fashion.

3. Become aware of any bodily sensations you feel. Just notice them and then let them go.

4. As you become aware of your thoughts, try not to attach any meaning to them or to judge them. They are just thoughts. Let them float by. Try not to have any expectations. Don't worry if your mind wanders; just gently bring it back to the present by focusing on your breathing for a moment.

Know that by doing this exercise, you are enhancing your health as well as learning a way to accept yourself because you accept whatever thoughts come up. Practice this meditation daily.

After you have completed this short mindfulness meditation, write in your journal about whatever came up for you: thoughts, feelings, or bodily sensations. Take time to explore them. Often the thoughts that surface are related to your childhood woundings and core beliefs. You might find some thoughts about yourself that were previously unknown to you.

The next mindfulness skill is about being in the moment during your daily activities. This informal mindfulness skill will help you slow down and come into the present moment. You will come to appreciate and enjoy your life much more by being mindful of the world around you.

Exercise 14: *Informal Mindfulness*

During any activity, stop and bring your awareness to what you are doing. For example, the next time you walk down the street, take a breath and notice everything as you walk. Feel your feet as they touch the ground. Notice each step. Feel your clothes move against your body. Notice the air as you breathe. Even notice your mood. Just be present and enjoy the moment. We are all too busy rushing around and not noticing the joy of the world around us. You can practice informal mindfulness as you engage in all sorts of activities. Here are a few of mine:

- Walking anywhere, for example in the woods or down the street

- Riding a horse

- Taking a shower

- Grocery shopping

- Eating

Now make a list in your journal of when you could practice mindfulness.

You can also use informal mindfulness to accomplish a goal. Say you are actively trying to lose weight for health reasons. You can use mindfulness when you are making your grocery list. As you write your list, feel the pencil in your hand and the pressure on the paper as you write, pay attention to the thoughts and feelings you are having, and feel your body as you write. Are you standing? Feel your weight on your legs and feet. Are you sitting? Feel your body against the chair or sofa. Breathe, relax, and just take it all in. Or perhaps you are walking down the aisles in the grocery store. Notice the color, smell, texture, and size of each item you select. Feel your hands on the grocery cart and the pressure you exert pushing it. Notice the wheels as they turn. Again, take it all in. Notice any thoughts you have. Just let them be, without attaching anything to them. They are just thoughts.

When you prepare your food, feel the texture and notice the smell. And when you are eating, be mindful of each bite. Eat slowly and notice how it smells, how it feels in your mouth, and how it tastes. Notice your feelings. Are you anxious, worried, depressed? Are you hungry?

Mindfulness helps us change our life traps because it teaches us not to judge our thoughts. But it is just as important to accurately interpret our thoughts and beliefs. Those of us with negative core beliefs tend to interpret our world in a fearful and distorted way, and this causes us to respond in unhealthful, negative ways. You have already learned how your core beliefs affect your dating choices. It is imperative that you learn how to manage your fearful or distorted thoughts so you can accurately assess and interpret your partner's behaviors. The next skill—realistic thinking— will teach you this.

Realistic Thinking

Realistic thinking, also called "rational thinking," is another important skill. It is a highly effective cognitive skill that was developed by famous pioneering cognitive-behavioral psychologist Albert Ellis. *Realistic thinking* teaches you to accurately assess and interpret your environment by using targeted questions to challenge your thoughts. Fearful thoughts are almost always distorted. For example, if I fear people won't like me, when I meet a new person, I will assume that person doesn't like me, and I will interpret that person's behaviors as support for my belief. Then, for example, if that person is actually just shy and doesn't talk much, I may assume it's because he or she doesn't like me. In response, I may act unfriendly or avoid that person. I may have missed the opportunity to have a new friend because of my distorted thinking. But how do you know your thinking is distorted? Realistic thinking is the skill that will guide you.

Realistic thinking is not the same as positive thinking. "Positive thinking" is about keeping an optimistic attitude by thinking that the best of something will happen, not the worst. However, I feel it falls short because it doesn't offer any reassurance you can actually believe. Just saying "It will be all right" won't be believable when a problem continues. On the other hand, if you use *evidence* to accurately interpret a situation and assess why and how it will be all right, you are more likely to believe that and find reassurance. With realistic thinking, you ask yourself targeted questions and use your answers to help you evaluate or dispute a certain thought. You will likely come to a different interpretation and a much more balanced conclusion. Let me illustrate with an example from my practice. Remember Christy, who wanted to stop "stalking" her ex-boyfriend after she broke up with him? I used realistic thinking to help her think about the situation differently.

One day, Christy came to her appointment very upset, saying she had not slept well in three days because of what she had seen on social media. I had taught her the six stages of change, which she embraced, but she had hit an obstacle and things needed a little tweaking. Remember that she had a narcissistic boyfriend who had lied about his involvement with other women. He broke her heart—and she ended their relationship. Though she had only broken up with him three weeks earlier, she could see from the pictures and comments on social media that he had definitely moved on and was having a wonderful life, whereas she was devastated and lonely.

Her excessive rumination about this was affecting her day and night. Christy was waking up at night feeling anxious and unable to get back to sleep. At work the next day, she was a mess—tired, puffy eyed, and irritable. She was overwhelmed by intrusive thoughts about her ex, ranging from thinking she was a failure who would never find love to feeling anger at him for ruining everything.

After she finished her story, I told her I was going to teach her a way to evaluate the situation more realistically so she could conclude whether her ex really was having a great life and if she really was a failure. I first asked her to write down her fear as a statement at the top of a legal pad. She wrote, "Tony is having a great life." I then had her draw a line down the center of the page, making two columns. I told her to write down evidence that supported her statement "Tony is having a great life" in one column and evidence that refuted this in the other column. I then asked her, "What evidence do you have that Tony is having a great life?" She said she thought he was because she had seen pictures of Tony partying with friends on vacation at a beach. There was also a really cute girl in one of the pictures.

I explained that Tony's pictures were not *evidence* he was having a great life, only evidence that he was at a beach with friends. She paused a moment to ponder what I had just said, and then said she understood. I then asked if she had any other *evidence* that Tony was having this supposed great life. She did not, so then I asked, "What evidence do you have that Tony may not be having such a wonderful life?" She said she heard he'd lost his job because he got caught lying at work. She said he always tried to cut corners and get away with things. He never had the patience to pay his dues and climb the ladder. He wanted things fast.

I then asked if she thought that someone with his values and ethics would have a good life. She said no. So she wrote that down: "Tony lies and cuts corners. He is not well thought of at work, and he cannot hold a job."

"Anything else?" I asked. She said she had to lend him a lot of money to bail him out of one of his work deals that he botched. He had never paid her back. That was two years ago. He always promised to but never got around to it. After a while, he made her feel guilty for asking by saying, "Aren't we in this relationship together? Isn't your money my money?" She stopped asking for the money back, even though that meant she could not buy a new laptop and had to use his spare one after hers died.

After exhausting the fear that Tony was having such a great life because she saw him on social media having fun, it became evident to her that although there were pictures of him with friends on a beach, the reality was that he was goofing off with friends as usual, had lost his job, and probably would never amount to much. What's more, he was not the stable, stand-up kind of guy she could ever trust and build a future with. She said this helped her realize that she didn't want him back the way he was. He wasn't the man she had thought he was. Of course, she wished he was different, but she knew it was unlikely he would change based on his history.

I then asked her to write a conclusion or summary statement. She wrote, "It is unlikely he is having a great life, and it's more likely that he is being the same irresponsible guy he has always been." I explained that every time she had the intrusive thought about his wonderful life, she needed to repeat her concluding statement.

We could have stopped there, but I wanted to show her how to think about her fear at a deeper level (what I suspected was underneath her original thought about his wonderful life). I asked her to think what else about him having a great life might have bothered her. She admitted that even though she didn't really want to be with him, it bothered her to see him having fun when she was still so miserable. It brought up all sorts of fears about her future. We then went through the same technique about those thoughts, basically that she would be alone and never find love or happiness. The situation triggered the deep fear that she would always be alone, which was associated with her emotional deprivation life trap. In the end, she was able to realize that there was no evidence for those thoughts, because they were just fears, and fears are usually distortions. She had more evidence that she had qualities that would more likely assure her of finding a wonderful person to share her life with (but we would have to work on her attraction to narcissistic men). Then I told her that we would work on a plan to continue to improve her life so she could reach her goals.

Realistic thinking is different than positive thinking because it uses evidence to support its conclusions, not Pollyanna platitudes. Using realistic thinking, you can have faith in the truth of your conclusions because they are based in evidence. Now you can practice this skill with the following exercise.

Exercise 15: *Realistic Thinking*

Think of something you have been worrying about recently. It may be an interaction with someone, or the likelihood of an unpleasant event, or that your partner is cheating on you. Follow the steps listed below.

1. Make your fearful thought into a statement. Write it at the top of a piece of paper or in your journal.

2. Use the questions below to help you think more realistically about your thought/fear statement. Make two columns under your statement; one column is evidence "for" your statement being true and the other is evidence "against" it being true. Write your answers in the appropriate column.

3. Begin with these questions:

   • What is the evidence for my statement being true?

   • What is the evidence against my statement being true?

4. Challenge each answer in the "for" and "against" columns with these questions:

   • Is this *always* true?

   • What are the odds (percentage) of this really happening or being true?

   • What alternative thoughts or views are there?

   • What is the very worst that can happen? What is so bad about that?

   • What logical errors (thinking errors) am I making?

   • What are the effects (advantages or disadvantages) of thinking this way?

   • Am I looking at the whole picture?

   • Am I being fully objective?

   • What would I tell a friend with this same thought in this same situation?

   • So what?

   • Is it really awful? Can I really not stand it?

   You will find that when you challenge the "for" answers, they will almost always be disproved; at the very least they will be unlikely. When you challenge the answers on the "against" side, they will almost always be proof against your thought/

fear statement, and that will reinforce your belief that your fear is unfounded.

5.   At the end, make a counterstatement from the evidence against your fearful thought that you can use whenever that unproductive, distorted fearful thought comes up again.

In summary, realistic thinking allows you to use your brain as a tool to accurately assess and interpret your thoughts based on evidence. Those of us with negative core beliefs must vigilantly challenge these distortions. By thinking realistically, you have more control over your thinking and your responses to distressing events.

Sometimes playing out your fear to the worst-case scenario is helpful. For example, perhaps you fear you will be let go in upcoming layoffs. You may be able to come up with evidence as to why it is unlikely that you would be laid off, but, of course, you have no control over the actual decision process. In this type of case, asking the question "So what?" or "Is it really that awful?" can help you to not catastrophize. Instead, you can accept that you can only do your best and trust that, although you wouldn't like it if you were laid off, you would survive—as evidenced, for example, by your being a smart, good networker and the fact that you already have your résumé prepared.

Combining realistic thinking with the practice of mindfulness, of being in the here and now instead of traveling to the past or future, is so valuable. Too often we ruminate on past mistakes, losses, or regrets or worry about something that may or not happen in the future. The truth is that the past is gone, and the future isn't here yet. Go ahead and make plans for the future or reflect on the past, but know that it is a waste of time and energy to stay upset or trapped by what happened in the past or what may happen in the future. In fact, your worrying today will have no effect on the past. It's gone. I tell the women I work with that the only thing of value that you can take from the past is a lesson. Worry is fear, and the only antidote to fear is reassurance. So should the thing you fear most happen, the best thing to say to yourself is that you will be able to handle it for reasons you've cited. I tell myself, *Okay, I really, really hope that does not happen, but if it does, I know I am smart, I have resources, and I have friends smarter than me, so I'll get through it.* And I usually add, *I won't like it, and I may feel devastated for a while, but I'll get through it. I will survive it.* Even if you don't think you will survive that thing you dread, I promise you will. You may not like it, and it may be devastating, but you will survive. People survive the most horrific tragedies. By reassuring yourself in this way, you'll survive anything the future throws at you. You can stop wasting time and energy worrying about it.

How to Change Your Life Traps

So far in this chapter, in addition to learning how change takes place (the six stages of change), you've learned several skills for actually changing your life traps: mindful breathing, mindfulness meditation, and realistic thinking. Now let's put all your building block skills together to see how you can change each life trap. I'll give a brief recap of the life trap's core beliefs and behaviors, list common thoughts you may have, offer actions or tasks that are meant both to specifically challenge the core beliefs that have trapped you and to help you break free from them, and provide affirmations that will help reinforce your resolve to change. All of these will work together to help you to change your life traps.

Changing the Life Trap of Abandonment

In the life trap of abandonment, you believe everyone will leave you. You worry about being rejected. To avoid being rejected, you may be clingy or jealous in your relationships. To control your fear of abandonment, you abruptly end your relationships, push others into ending them, or avoid relationships altogether. This includes any kind of relationship, not just romantic ones. You may have thoughts like these:

- *I don't trust people because I fear they will reject or leave me.*

- *I choose to be alone sometimes rather than risk being abandoned.*

- *I do whatever I can to keep someone in a relationship.*

- *Sometimes I manipulate a relationship into ending.*

You *can* break free of the life trap of abandonment. Here are some concrete actions you can take to free yourself:

- Initiate one conversation a day with a friend or coworker. It doesn't have to be long, just a minute or two. Slowly increase the time as you feel comfortable.

- Initiate one social activity a week. For example, ask someone to go out to eat, see a movie, go shopping, take a walk, go for a run, or attend a lecture. You can only build friendships that you can trust by spending time with others.

- Risk being vulnerable and ask for what you want or need rather than becoming jealous, possessive, or manipulative. Asking for what you need develops trust. Practice realistic thinking to see if your expectations are realistic ones.

To support yourself as you break free from your life trap, use affirmations to strengthen your resolve. Here are some affirmations you might use:

- I choose to take the risk and be vulnerable in order to change.

- I am courageous.

- I am changing.

Changing the Life Trap of Mistrust/Abuse

In the life trap of mistrust/abuse, you find it hard to believe that others won't hurt or mistreat you. You often feel helpless and powerless in your relationships. You may even believe that you deserve to be abused or mistreated. (Of course, this is *never* true.) You may have thoughts like these:

- *I don't trust people.*

- *I feel helpless and powerless.*

- *I deserve to be mistreated.*

Note: If you are a survivor of childhood or adult trauma and you have not worked through it with a therapist, proceed carefully with any exercise that asks you to delve into your thoughts and feelings. I worry about you and strongly recommend you go into treatment with a qualified therapist who works with trauma survivors. If you choose not to at this time, please be careful as you do these tasks. If you get upset, know that you can stop at any time. You can come back to these tasks when you like. But if you continually find you are having a strong and negative reaction, I recommend you seek treatment.

You *can* break free of the life trap of mistrust/abuse. Here are some concrete actions you can take to free yourself:

- Develop a support list of trustworthy friends, family, and/or coworkers.

- Pick one person from your list and initiate a conversation. Maybe you have seen this person be kind or empathic to others. Continue to develop a closer relationship by learning about that person and slowly sharing more of yourself. Go as slowly as you need; just keep going. Eventually, you may share your fears of mistrust. It doesn't mean you have to share about your abuse or trauma history. It just means you let the person know you are taking a risk to become friends.

- Do small household tasks every day to increase your sense of control. Organize a drawer, clean and organize a closet, or make your bed every day.

- Ask someone for help with a problem or to help you fix something at home or at work. From this, you will learn that there are people you can trust.

To support yourself as you break free from your life trap, use affirmations to strengthen your resolve. Here are some affirmations you might use:

- I can protect myself.

- I have trustworthy friends.

- I am in control.

Changing the Life Trap of Emotional Deprivation

In the life trap of emotional deprivation, you feel that no one understands you, and you believe there is no one you can count on. You also believe you have nothing of value or interest to offer. You feel ashamed of yourself and feel as if you don't fit in. Your distorted image of yourself hinders you from connecting with others in a meaningful way. You may have thoughts like these:

- *I can't count on anyone to be there for me.*

- *I am boring and have nothing of interest to say or offer to others.*

- *No one understands me.*

- *I give more than I take.*

- *I am afraid to let people take care of me.*

You *can* break free of the life trap of emotional deprivation. Here are some concrete actions you can take to free yourself:

- Give yourself one nice thing every day: a flower, a special cup of coffee, a book, a new robe, new gloves, or a library card. You might buy something frivolous for yourself, such as a beautiful scarf you don't need but just like and want.

- Make a list of twenty-five of your positive attributes. Don't ask anyone to help you. They can be as simple as "I am a good listener," "I won the sportsmanship award in college for track," or "I am a loyal friend."

- When you're not feeling well, call someone and ask for help. Let that person take care of you, buy you juice or soup, and come over to help.

- Share something you feel ashamed about with a trusted person.

To support yourself as you break free from your life trap, use affirmations to strengthen your resolve. Here are some affirmations you might use:

- I am valuable.

- I am interesting.

- I am worthy of love.

Changing the Life Trap of Defectiveness/Shame

In the life trap of defectiveness/shame, you are convinced that something is inherently wrong with you. You're not sure what it is, but you know that some part of you is horribly flawed. You feel so ashamed of yourself that you don't believe you deserve to be loved. You likely put on an act around others so they can't see the "real" you. You may have thoughts like these:

- *I am horribly flawed.*

- *I am a fake.*

- *I'm worthless.*

You *can* break free of the life trap of defectiveness/shame. Here are some concrete actions you can take to free yourself:

- Treat yourself with kindness and respect each day.

- Do one thing each day to feel good about yourself.

- Achieve one thing each day (for example, go to the gym, buy groceries for the week, or organize your closet).

- Value your time: don't give it all away.

- Value your future: save money for your retirement, open a savings account, open an IRA.

To support yourself as you break free from your life trap, use affirmations to strengthen your resolve. Here are some affirmations you might use:

- I am unique and valuable.

- I love and respect myself.

Changing the Life Trap of Subjugation

In the life trap of subjugation, you are trapped in the belief that unless you meet the demands and needs of others, they won't love or care about you. You believe you have no choice but to go along with whatever others want. You avoid being assertive for fear that someone will withhold love or things that you need. As a result, you don't ask for what you need, voice your opinion, or disagree with anyone. You may have thoughts like these:

- *I feel afraid to say no to someone.*

- *I let others control me.*

- *I always do what is asked of me.*

You *can* break free of the life trap of subjugation. Here are some concrete actions you can take to free yourself:

- Before you do something, practice asking yourself these questions: *Why am I doing this? Who benefits? Do I want to do it? How do I feel about doing it? Am I enjoying myself?* This will help increase your awareness as to why you are doing something.

- Practice assertiveness by offering your opinion. Start with something simple. For example, if a friend or coworker suggests a movie, a restaurant, or an activity, before you agree, suggest a different one. The point is not to be disagreeable but to experience voicing a different opinion. The other person may not agree with you, but that is not the point. The point is to speak up and not be silent.

- Ask someone to explain something to you. For example, you can ask a waiter at a restaurant to explain the specials, a salesperson to explain a product, or a coworker to explain a project or document. Again, the point is to begin speaking up and asking for things.

To support yourself as you break free from your life trap, use affirmations to strengthen your resolve. Here are some affirmations you might use:

- I am entitled to my opinion.

- I ask for what I want and need.

- I choose what I want to do.

Changing the Life Trap of Self-Sacrifice

In the life trap of self-sacrifice, you are trapped in the belief that you need to help or fix others. The problem is you get so involved in helping others that you neglect yourself. Sometimes resentment creeps in, but your guilt quickly quashes your feeling of resentment. You may have thoughts like these:

- *I feel so sorry for others if they are suffering or in need. I just want to help them.*

- *I feel guilty if I put myself first, fail to help others, or feel any resentment.*

- *I don't like to disappoint others.*

You *can* break free of the life trap of self-sacrifice. Here are some concrete actions you can take to free yourself:

- Practice saying no. Try saying, "I'll get back to you" or "I'll have to check." This buys you time to say no.

- When you feel the urge to help or fix others, instead ask them, "What do you think you're going to do?" This helps them come up with solutions instead of you. Then just be quiet and resist the urge to speak. You actually do others a disservice when you take over for them. It is better to set a boundary and detach with love and kindness. Remind yourself that you are still helping them. It is sort of the same idea as teaching them to fish instead of giving them a fish; this way they can learn to feed themselves.

To support yourself as you break free from your life trap, use affirmations to strengthen your resolve. Here are some affirmations you might use:

- Taking care of myself is healthy.

- I help others best when I allow them to seek solutions to their own problems.

- Disappointment is a normal part of life.

Changing the Life Trap of Unrelenting Standards

In the life trap of unrelenting standards, you are stuck in the belief that what you do or have is not good enough, so you keep trying harder and harder to attain your unrealistic goals. Maybe they are your goals, or maybe they are someone else's. Maybe you are trying to win that other person's approval. This life trap has three types: achievement oriented (workaholic), status oriented (must have the best), and compulsivity oriented (slave to perfection and perfect order). You may have all three or some combination thereof. You must accomplish your goals, even at the cost of your health and well-being. You work hard and exercise hard. You think exercising hard is relaxation, but it isn't. You don't know how to relax. Your work-life balance is out of whack. You may have thoughts like these:

- *When I try to relax, I feel I am being lazy.*

- *I don't enjoy things that I have worked so hard to achieve or attain.*

- *I know my health is suffering. I sleep and eat poorly and don't exercise.*

You *can* break free of the life trap of unrelenting standards. Here are some concrete actions you can take to free yourself:

- Take a day off and do whatever feels fun. Make it a free day with nothing you *have* to do, no pressure, no deadlines. Do not check work e-mail or return work-related phone calls.

- Practice informal mindfulness as you go about this free day: use all your senses to notice your bodily sensations and everything around you.

- Include mindful breathing as you go about your day. Remember, doing nothing is doing something. It's called relaxation, and relaxation is very important to your health and well-being.

- During your free day, notice if any thoughts or worries come up for you. Write them down and then use your realistic thinking to work through each one.

- Throughout your day, remind yourself why you are doing this— for example, to learn to relax, to help my work-life balance, and to increase my health and well-being. At the end of the day, give yourself kudos for having done it and notice if you enjoyed your day.

To support yourself as you break free from your life trap, use affirmations to strengthen your resolve. Here are some affirmations you might use:

- I choose to have balance in my life.

- Relaxing strengthens me by healing my body and soul.

- I choose to enjoy my life.

I hope this helps you see how you can use the skills in this chapter to change your life traps. Return to this section often for encouragement and guidance as you work to change your life traps.

Putting It All Together

In this chapter, we focused on the building blocks to change your life traps. You learned the six stages of behavioral change: precontemplation, contemplation, preparation/determination, activation, maintenance, and relapse. You can use these stages to help you make a plan to change a particular negative behavior associated with your life trap. We talked about the difference between a slip and relapse, that a slip is a momentary lapse while a relapse is a sustained one. Relapses, though frustrating, are part of the cycle of change, and when you have one, remind yourself you had the courage to try to change, which in itself is a step toward change. You learned that the key to succeeding in changing behavior is to have specific targeted goals and to identify every obstacle that might derail you and then make a plan for each. We also covered the benefits of mindfulness and how to practice mindful breathing as well as mindfulness meditation. These two skills help you change your life traps by teaching you to be less judgmental of yourself, increasing self-acceptance, and helping you to not be held prisoner by your negative thoughts. You also learned about realistic thinking, a skill that can help you to assess and evaluate your thoughts and responses as well as to change your life trap by challenging your negative thoughts. You will use this important skill when you assess a potential partner; using realistic thinking can make the difference between picking another narcissist and picking a nice guy (more about this in chapter 8). All the skills in this chapter complement each other. At the end of this chapter, examples illustrated how you could put all these skills together to change your life traps. These skills, which you will learn, develop, and integrate into your life, will help you to think differently about yourself as well as behave diffferently. This will enable you to change your unhealthy pattern of repeating narcissistic relationships and to have the relationship you deserve.

Now let's move on to chapter 7. There you will learn about the benefits of self-care and how to implement a self-care plan.

CHAPTER 7

Self-Care: Becoming Your
Own Fairy Godmother

If you have neglected yourself for a long time, it can be challenging to take care of yourself. If you have internalized negative messages from childhood and engaged in unhealthy ways of thinking and behaving, you may feel selfish if you think of and care for yourself. You may find it so uncomfortable that you slide back into peacekeeping or people-pleasing mode. But as you work on healing from relationships with narcissists, as you learn to nurture and honor yourself, you will come to understand that healthy self-love is *not* selfish—and it is a prerequisite for having a healthy relationship. Treating yourself with kindness, respect, and compassion demonstrates to others that you are of value and deserve to be treated with respect. Healthy self-love means loving and accepting yourself for the person you are. Compassionately setting boundaries and limits—how much you are capable of doing for others while taking good care of yourself—will help you create a healthy, reciprocal relationship. Now is the time to become your own fairy godmother *and* the princess by using the fairy dust of self-care.

Essential Elements

In this chapter, you will learn self-care techniques to practice in all areas of your life. These will help you heal from the effects of your life traps. The first involves what I call the "triad of wellness"—eating well, getting enough sleep, and exercising—and understanding how it provides a sturdy foundation upon which to build good physical and mental health. You will also learn about compassionate boundaries and limit setting, as well as how to recognize reciprocal relationships. And you will identify your values, which are your "rudder" when dating because they keep you on a straight course. Taking care of your emotional and physical needs by incorporating a self-care regimen will lay the foundation for a healthy lifestyle. When you feel strong mentally and physically, you will not allow another to take advantage of you. Let's get started.

The Triad of Wellness

"Triad of wellness" is a phrase I use to describe three fundamental components of self-care that I believe are the foundation of good physical and mental health: nutrition, exercise, and sleep. Having them in balance is key to your well-being. Let's begin with nutrition.

Nutrition: Eating for Health

As women, we get caught up with what and how much we eat in order to achieve a certain outcome. For too many of us, it is to lose weight. Some of us even do "destination weight loss," meaning we have a beach vacation, reunion, wedding, or some other event for which we need to lose fifteen to twenty pounds. Once the event is over or even while at the event, especially once we are on vacation, we begin eating (and drinking) our unhealthy way again. Sound familiar? Food is great. I am a foodie. But I had to learn to eat for health and not for weight loss.

Giving our body healthy foods is necessary to our health and optimal functioning. When we take the time to buy the healthiest foods, prepare them, and feed ourselves, it is an act of self-care. It says we value ourselves. Eating the right amount of food—not over- or undereating—makes you feel good and in control.

Try to eat the healthiest whole food you can afford. Avoid sugary and processed foods (usually carbohydrate laden) that offer no nutritional value. Carbohydrates, like sugar, turn to glucose in your bloodstream and increase your blood sugar. When your blood sugar drops, you will feel a craving for carbohydrates. It becomes a vicious cycle of craving and overeating. I have found that the more sugar I eat, the more I crave it. I especially noticed it when I got into the habit of having a sugary snack at 3:00 p.m. What is it with 3:00 p.m. on a workday? If I had a cookie (or worse) at that time, my body came to expect it every day. I broke the habit by eating a handful of almonds instead (about thirty almonds). It took about a week, but my body adjusted. Nuts of any kind help keep your blood sugar even because they contain monounsaturated fat and protein and that prevents cravings. Now I keep almonds in my office and in my car. Whenever I feel hungry between meals, or if I am running late for a meal, it is the perfect snack. Try it.

While we're on the topic of food and eating, I want to say something about loss of appetite. You may experience this if you've just broken up with someone or if you are under a lot of stress. If I am under a little stress, I stress-eat. But if I am devastated over something, I totally lose my appetite. Although loss of appetite may be a normal response to loss, grief, depression, or anxiety, it is not healthy if you have a sustained loss of appetite. If this happens, you must still get nutrition into your body. Try drinking whole milk if you are not lactose intolerant. Whole milk is a complete food. It has proteins, fat, carbohydrates, vitamins A, D, E, and K, and the minerals iron, calcium, and phosphorus. If you can't drink milk or prefer not to, then drink your nutrients another way. Try a smoothie made with yogurt and whole fruits and ideally some greens or protein powder. Or you could use soy, coconut, or almond milk. The point is that when your body is under significant stress and you lose your appetite, you still need to attend to your nutritional needs. Besides being unhealthy, eating the wrong foods when you are under stress—the carbohydrates and foods with high sugar content—result in fatigue and leave you less able to handle the stress you are under.

Loss of appetite can also be an attempt to control your body. It is usually in response to your environment—a situation or a particular person who makes you feel out of control. This can become a serious problem. If you fit this description, I recommend you seek treatment from your primary care physician and a dietician, or consult with a psychologist.

Healthy eating is important to our well-being because its focus is on health, not weight. Eating balanced, healthy meals at regular intervals each day—instead of skipping meals, eating foods high in carbohydrates and sugar, or indulging in too much alcohol or caffeine—helps us manage our stress better. Choosing to eat healthy foods is a way of valuing ourselves. Let's try a couple of exercises to help you eat healthily.

Exercise 16: *Mindful Nutrition*

Go to a farmers' market and peruse the fresh fruits and vegetables. Use the skill of mindfulness you learned in chapter 7. Really be present—be in the moment and take it all in. Sample the fare. Smell the freshness. Buy yourself a perfectly ripe piece of fruit and savor its fresh flavor. Remind yourself, *Eating healthfully is within my control and taking control will empower me.*

Exercise 17: *Mindful Eating*

Now that you've bought some wonderful, healthy foods at the farmers' market, it is important to be mindful when you eat those good foods. Eating mindfully will help you eat slowly, savor your food, and avoid overeating, which can lead to indigestion. To learn the practice of mindful eating, let's start with something simple—a piece of fruit.

Select a piece of fruit. If it needs to be washed before being eaten, notice how the water feels as you wash it. Then sit someplace comfortable where there are no distractions: no television, radio, music, reading, talking on the telephone, or other activities. As you eat your piece of fruit, observe everything about it: its texture, smell, and taste. Also, mindfully eat each bite with the intention to take care of your body. Enjoy the silence while you eat. Think of where you just bought the food you are eating: maybe the farmers' market. Wonder about who grew it, what was its journey to you.

You can practice mindfulness with any meal. You will find that, as you practice mindful eating, you develop a greater appreciation of your food.

Mindfulness can be practiced even while you are preparing a meal. You can notice the weight and feel of the utensils you use to prepare the food, notice the aromas as it's cooking, observe the change in texture or color as you cook it. Mindfulness of eating and preparing food keeps you in the present moment. It is relaxing and healing, both of which are components of good self-care.

Keeping your body toned and strong is just as important as giving it the nutrients it needs. That is where exercise comes in.

Exercise: Working Out for Life

Working out will improve your physical and emotional health and enhance your well-being. Regular exercise strengthens your body, mind, and soul. It improves your mood as well as your cardiovascular system. In exercising, you are literally working out for life.

Regular exercise can help protect you from many health problems, such as stroke, type 2 diabetes, arthritis, high blood pressure, high cholesterol, and obesity. It can also help prevent gaining that extra five, ten, fifteen, or twenty pounds!

Exercise improves your mood by the production of specific chemicals in the brain that are associated with happiness. Ever hear of "runner's high"? It's true; I've experienced it many times. But you don't have to run a marathon to feel it—just a brisk walk will work. You may find that your self-confidence and self-esteem increase as you get in better shape, lose weight, and develop better muscle tone. Also, when you exercise you will find that you have more energy afterward because exercise gives your heart and lungs a workout. This causes them to work together more efficiently. The result? You have more energy! But when you are ready to sleep at night, having exercised during the day promotes better quality sleep; you fall asleep easier, sleep deeper, and stay asleep longer.

Cardiovascular exercise (aerobic exercise) can help with your brain functioning. A common phrase among physicians is "heart health equals brain health." This is because when your heart is working more efficiently, it increases certain chemicals in the brain that improve memory and learning. It can also help your brain make new brain cells, which will help prevent brain shrinkage. Brain shrinkage is associated with Alzheimer's disease, a progressive disease that destroys memory.

So, there are lots of good reasons to exercise—and you don't have to commit a lot of time to an exercise regimen to reap the benefits. Studies have shown that walking briskly ten minutes a day can have health benefits, including weight loss even when you have not changed your diet.

If exercise was something you gave up in your relationship with a narcissist or if you had a lapse for any other reason, begin slowly. Start with walking three to four times a week; it's the easiest and least expensive form of exercise. You don't need to join a fitness center, and the only equipment you need is a decent pair of athletic shoes. I tell the women I work with to walk out their front door and walk fifteen minutes in one direction and then fifteen minutes back. You can bring your coffee, tea, water, or whatever with you. You can bring your phone and use the time to call a supportive friend or family member. It is also a perfect time to practice informal mindfulness. Making exercise a regular part of your self-care regimen is another way to value yourself.

A *note about safety:* Always pay attention to your surroundings if you are exercising outside alone. If you feel unsafe or vulnerable walking alone, ask a friend to join you, join a walking group in your area, or use exercise videos at home instead of walking. Cable stations offer many programmed fitness routines.

A *note about motivation:* If you struggle with the motivation to exercise, I recommend using the buddy system. If you have someone you can walk or exercise with, that's great. But if not, you can call a friend before and after your walk or workout. Having to check in with someone helps you stay on a regular fitness regimen. Another way to stay motivated is to use a wrist monitor, an app, or some other technical gadget to monitor your fitness. Really, we have no excuse not to exercise for fifteen minutes a day three to four times a week. *Remember, before you start any exercise regimen, always check with your physician.*

Working out is a commitment to yourself and your life. The following exercise will help you commit to be fit for life.

Exercise 18: *Commit to Be Fit*

Use the checklist below to help you begin your commitment to be fit for life. Adjust the checklist to your personal circumstances, adding (or deleting) items as needed. (A downloadable version of this checklist can be found at http://www.newharbinger.com /33674, if you'd like to print it out. Just follow the prompts on the site to access it.)

1. Take inventory of your workout clothes and shoes.

    ☐ athletic shoes

    ☐ comfortable clothes for exercise

    ☐ yoga mat or other exercise equipment (ball, jump rope, or other equipment)

2. Write in your journal your commitment to exercise.

    ☐ I want to be fit.

    ☐ I want to feel good about my body.

    ☐ I want to feel stronger.

3. Develop a plan, write it in your journal, and post it where you'll see it every day.

    ☐ I will walk fifteen minutes a day, three times a week.

    ☐ At work, I'll park the car at the far end of the parking lot and walk from there.

    ☐ I'll take the stairs instead of the elevator.

    ☐ I'll walk five minutes a day, three times a week. Each week I'll add five minutes until I reach thirty minutes, three times a week.

4. Find support.

    ☐ I'll ask a friend to walk with me.

    ☐ I'll see if I can join a friend at the gym three times a week.

    ☐ I'll take a yoga class.

    ☐ I'll get an electronic heart monitor, or an exercise app.

Nutrition and exercise are the first two components of the triad of wellness. The last component is sleep.

Sleep: Resting for Rejuvenation and Repair

Sleep is much more than a beauty aid. Regular and quality sleep is critical to healthy functioning. Most of us don't get enough sleep on a regular basis. Adults need about seven hours of sleep a night. Getting less than this amount over consecutive nights is diagnosed as insomnia. (Insomnia refers to difficulty falling asleep or staying asleep.) According to the *DSM-V*, population-based estimates indicate that about one-third of US adults report insomnia symptoms. A Mayo Clinic staff member writes on the Mayo Clinic website: "Sleep is as important to your health as a healthy diet and regular exercise.... People with insomnia report a lower quality of life compared with people who are sleeping well."[18]

Ironically, science seems to know more about what sleep deprivation leads to than what sleep actually does for us. But they have found that our brains are quite active during sleep, repairing or shutting down neurons that were used or depleted during awake time. Sleep science is a very interesting topic, but let's get a little more personal here and look at reasons why you might not be getting a good night's sleep.

For most people, and you may be one of these people, it is due to worry, anxiety, or depression. It can also be due to medical issues, such as chronic pain, perimenopause or menopause, gastroesophageal reflux disease (GERD), or overactive thyroid, to name a few. It is always important to rule out medical reasons for your sleep problems.

Studies have shown that even partial sleep deprivation can have a significant effect on mood. University of Pennsylvania researcher Jared D. Minkel and his associates found that subjects who were limited to only 4.5 hours of sleep a night for one week reported feeling more stressed, angry, sad, and mentally exhausted. When the subjects resumed normal sleep, they reported a dramatic improvement in mood.[19] If you are recovering from yet another narcissistic relationship, you are probably experiencing sleep difficulty. Getting consistent and sufficient quality sleep each night will help you face the challenges of another breakup.

Not only can lack of sleep affect your mood, but your mood can also affect your sleep. Anxiety and stress increase agitation and arousal, which make it hard to sleep because you are awake and alert, and depression can cause rumination, which interferes with sleep. Although too little sleep is a problem, too much sleep, hypersomnia, can also be a problem.

Hypersomnia

In contrast with insomnia, some of you may experience *hypersomnia*, which is defined by the *Diagnostic and Statistical Manual of Mental Disorders* (5th edition) as excessive sleepiness, evidenced by either prolonged sleep episodes or daytime sleep episodes that occur at least three times a week for at least three months.[20] If you sleep a lot, it could indicate you are avoiding a painful situation or emotion. If this has been going on for quite a while, it might be time to check with a therapist or your physician. If, on the other hand, you are just staying up too late and therefore having difficulty waking in the morning, a simple solution is to put your alarm clock across the room so you have to get up to turn it off—and then turn on lights to wake yourself up. Of course, the best and healthiest solution is to go to bed at a reasonable hour and get sufficient sleep every night.

Sleep Hygiene

Sleep hygiene refers to ways to help you obtain healthy (or "good") sleep.

One aspect of sleep hygiene involves putting yourself on a sleep schedule by going to bed around the same time every night and getting up about the same time in the morning. This schedule will set your internal clock, which regulates your sleep cycle. Once your internal clock is set, your brain will wake up your body at the same time every morning. You will also get sleepy around the same time every night. Maintain your bedtime and waking times even on the weekends.

To help yourself wind down in the evening, consider turning the lights down, taking a warm bath or shower, or reading. Avoid exercising too close to bedtime, eating a heavy meal too late in the evening, drinking alcoholic beverages late at night (alcohol raises your blood sugar, and when it drops a few hours later, you'll wake up), or drinking caffeinated drinks at night. If you are sensitive to caffeine, you may need to avoid caffeinated drinks from midafternoon on (or even earlier, depending on your level of sensitivity). Also, avoid engaging in activities that will arouse you, such as watching anxiety-provoking TV shows or movies, paying your bills at night, or getting into an emotional discussion or argument late at night. In general, avoid TV and other screen time (computer, smartphone, and other electronic devices) too close to bedtime.

Exercise 19: *Sweet Dreams*

Get out your journal. Take a minute to think about sleep hygiene. What is your sleep hygiene like now? What you would like your evening ritual, your sleep hygiene, to look like? Write it out. Try it out over the next week and make any tweaks necessary. Make notes in your journal of what did or did not work.

Worry Pad

We all wake up at times during the night. This may be due to worries or concerns, or we may just need to use the bathroom. If you are prone to waking up with worrisome thoughts or fears and can't get back to sleep, a neat tip is to use a worry pad, a place where you can list your worries. Keep something to write on—a pad of paper or notebook—and a pen or pencil next to your bed. When you wake up at night, just lean over and write down a couple of words that will remind you of your thought, fear, or concern. For example, if you're concerned about a report or call you have to make at work, write "check report" or "call so-and-so," but do not turn on the light because that will wake up your brain. Then tell yourself that, since you've written it down, you don't have to keep trying to remember it, and you'll address it the next day, after you've had a good night's sleep. Once you've written it down and reassured yourself that you'll attend to it in the morning, it doesn't have to keep nagging you. I find that if I don't write it down, it keeps looping in my mind, keeping me awake. If you are unsure what's bothering you but keep waking up, another great technique to use is visualization.

Visualization

Visualization is creating a mental image of a scene in your mind. This is a wonderful technique that works well. I used to teach it to recovering substance abusers who couldn't sleep. Without substances, the reason why they started using in the first place would percolate in their minds all night. They could not take narcotics, so I taught them this technique, and it worked for all of them. If it worked for them, it will work for you. But like any new skill, it takes consistent practice. You can't use this one night and then not again for days or weeks.

You'll have a chance to use the visualization technique in exercise 21 below, but first you'll need to do a little preparation for it by recalling a place where you felt safe. I'll give a little background information first; then in exercise 20, you will "find" your safe place. To begin, think of a scene from your childhood when you felt safe and relaxed—perhaps it's the beach, summer camp, your backyard, holidays at your grandmother's house, or a tree you used to climb. It's important to use a scene from childhood because it was a time when you did not have all the problems of adulthood (relationships, finances, work, family, and so on). Even if you had an abusive childhood or adolescence, try to identify a place where you felt safe—perhaps at a friend's house or someplace outdoors. If you cannot recall a place where you felt safe and relaxed as a child, make up a scene of safety. Some people picture meadows or woods or the beach. Take a few moments now to find your safe place in the exercise below. Have your journal or a piece of paper and a pen ready.

Exercise 20: *Finding Your Safe Place*

Find a comfortable place to sit quietly. Become conscious of your breath and breathe mindfully. Feel your body and mind relax.

Now think of a time and place in your childhood when you felt safe and happy. Or, if your childhood was very difficult, create a scene where you feel safe now. Perhaps it's by a stream, in a beautiful garden, or at the home of a friend. It may be an imaginary place or a real place.

Bring your scene, your safe place, up into your consciousness. What is the context of the scene? Recall exactly what you used to think and feel, or what you think and feel now when you are in your safe place. Rest in your safe place for a few moments.

Now, turn to your journal. Make notes to remind you of your safe place. Describe it and how you felt when you were there—or how you feel now when you are there. This is the safe place you will return to whenever you use visualization.

Whichever scene you choose, use it each time you do the visualization technique. (However, you can try another if you find a scene isn't working.) The principle behind this technique and the use of the same scene is that you are pairing your scene with relaxation. Your body learns that association so that just bringing your scene into your mind's eye will cause your body to relax.

Visualization can be used to relax anytime, so why don't you try this exercise now? (For your practice, you don't have to lie down—though you can, if you want. Instead, you can sit somewhere quiet and comfortable.) Becoming familiar with the process will allow you to return to it at night when you're having trouble sleeping.

Exercise 21: *A Way to Sleep: Visualizing Your Safe Place*

Lie in bed in a comfortable position and then bring your awareness to your breathing. Breathe deeply and mindfully in a comfortable rhythm, focusing on each breath.

Gently, bring up your scene and let yourself feel the safeness of that place.

Now, very slowly, go through your safe place using each of your five senses: sight, sound, touch, smell, and taste.

Look around you, and take everything in…

Listen for any sounds…the wind through the trees…the creek flowing over rocks.… If it is very quiet, listen for the sounds in the quiet…

Touch…the earth…a tree…your cat—whatever or whoever is present in your safe place.

Take a deep breath and notice the smells around you, or various aromas around you… Remember the smells associated with the scene you chose.

Finally, taste…the salt in the air or in the water at the beach…a blade of grass…a sun-warmed strawberry. Take the taste of your safe place deeply in.

If you find yourself thinking about some problem, worry, or concern, don't be alarmed. This is normal. Just gently bring your awareness back to your breathing and start again, using your five senses to ground you in your safe place.

Let yourself rest quietly in this safe haven. Continue to breathe deeply and mindfully. Soon, as your mind and body relax, you will gently drift off to sleep…

As you work with visualization, especially when you're using visualization to get to sleep or return to sleep, try to avoid frustration, as that only serves to wake you up. And remember that it is normal to have problems, worries, and concerns arise during visualization. Let them be and just simply and gently return your awareness to your breathing and your safe place. Be patient with yourself, and sleep will come.

Committing to the triad of wellness is one aspect of self-care, of becoming your own fairy godmother. And as your own fairy godmother, you have bestowed upon yourself the gift of health through nutrition, exercise, and sleep.

Boundaries, Limits, and Values

If you're a visual learner like me, mental images help you learn, so I like to use the metaphor of a boat to explain boundaries, limits, and values. The hull of a boat protects you from the sea, just as your boundaries protect you from the negative behaviors and demands of others. The two oars that guide a boat's movement are like the two words "yes" and "no" that make up your limits. They determine how much you can do for others ("yes") while still taking care of yourself ("no"). The rudder keeps the boat oriented in the direction you want, similar to your values, which keep you aligned (how you think and act) with the things that mean the most to you.

Having healthy boundaries, knowing your limits, and living your values will protect you from repeating another narcissistic relationship. In this section, we'll take a closer look at each of these important qualities. Let's start with boundaries.

Boundaries: Separation and Protection from Others

Boundaries are the imaginary barriers you create around yourself to separate and protect you from others. They determine what you will or will not accept in terms of other people's behaviors or demands upon you. We have many types of boundaries—personal, physical, professional, and spiritual. Because of their important role in relationships, and particularly in avoiding relationships with narcissists—we'll be focusing here on your personal and physical boundaries.

Your *physical boundaries* include your body and your personal space. You determine how physically close you want to be to someone and how you want to share your body with another person. Violations of your physical boundaries can be, for example, inappropriate touching or someone standing too close to you during a conversation.

Personal boundaries include your sense of self, your opinions, and your beliefs. All these make up your identity—what you stand for, who you are. Violations of your personal boundaries can be someone demanding you do something against your beliefs, such as going out with a married man, or not respecting your time, such as insisting that you do something like host a last-minute dinner party even though you are exhausted from work and just want to relax. Violations of personal boundaries can also be someone reading your personal e-mails or texts.

Having healthy boundaries means you have clearly defined your boundaries to yourself and others. When you have healthy boundaries, you don't let people violate them, and if they do, you stand up for yourself and firmly tell them you won't tolerate this kind of behavior. Standing up for yourself demonstrates that you respect yourself and that you expect others to respect you as well.

You cannot have a healthy relationship without healthy boundaries. If you have unhealthy boundaries, you can lose yourself by putting the needs and demands of others ahead of your own. Here are a few examples of unhealthy boundaries: relying solely on your partner for your happiness and in order to feel complete, giving in to all of your partner's demands and not asking for anything that you need, needing to be with your partner at all times because you are unable to be alone, or allowing yourself to be controlled by your partner, so you stop seeing friends or family because your partner wants all your attention. Unhealthy boundaries, therefore, contribute to your repeated involvement in relationships with narcissists because you allow the narcissist to take advantage of or to exploit you. Learning to compassionately set boundaries is an important component of self-care. It is taking care of yourself. Healthy boundaries protect you from others taking advantage of you.

You weren't born with boundaries, healthy or otherwise. They are something you developed and learned. When you were a child, if those around you—parents, caregivers, siblings, or others—did not respect your body, your personal space, your needs, and your beliefs and opinions, you probably never developed healthy boundaries. For example, if your time was not valued, you let the demands of others dictate how you spent your time; if your body was not respected, you allowed your body to be touched inappropriately; if your beliefs and opinions were ridiculed or ignored, you accepted others' opinions and did not offer your own. As a result, your lack of boundaries was a problem not only when you were a child but also when you became an adult, especially when it came to dating and rela-tionships. Because you lacked healthy boundaries, you easily became involved with narcissists because narcissists know exactly what they want and have no problem demanding it from others—and you would be only too accommodating. Since healthy boundaries are so important, let's look at how to create them.

Exercise 22: *Create Healthy Boundaries*

Carefully consider each of the items below, taking time to reflect on how these situations or experiences may look in your own life. Don't rush. Write your reflections and answers in your journal. You may want to return to this exercise more than once.

1. Find a quiet place to sit and think of past and current situations when you let others take advantage of you. Maybe you allowed them to have you do something you didn't really want to do. Examples:

   - I gave up going to the gym because my partner wanted me to spend time with him.
   - I stopped seeing friends because my partner didn't like them.
   - I allowed my partner to decide how I dressed, what I read, and so on.
   - I let my partner yell at me.
   - I accept blame for things I did not do.

2. Make a list of what things you will no longer tolerate from others. Examples:

   - No one can tell me what I am feeling.
   - No one can tell me how to spend my time.
   - No one will demand intimacy from me if I am not ready.
   - I will not tolerate someone yelling at me.
   - I will no longer accept blame for things I did not do.

3. Decide what you need for personal or emotional space. Examples:

   - I need a thirty-minute transition time when I come home from work.
   - I need time to myself on the weekends.
   - I need a room of my own or privacy to do yoga, work, or read.

Make a plan of what you will say or do if people do violate your boundary. Here are some actions you could take:

- I will tell them they have disrespected my boundary.

- I will tell them I will not tolerate that behavior.

- If they push back or get defensive, I will walk away or remove myself from the situation. I can then write them a note, letter, e-mail, or text, telling them what they did and how I will not tolerate it, reiterating my boundary, and saying that if they continue with that violation in the future I will not continue to see them (and if they are family or work-related people, I will follow my instructions below).

4. Make a list of the people you will tell about your boundaries—what you will tolerate, what space you need, and so on. Examples:

- *My mother:* I will no longer tolerate her demands on my time on the telephone. Talking for one to two hours a day is too much. I will tell her that I need to hang up, and if she continues to ignore my request, I will politely say I am hanging up, and then hang up.

- *My brother:* I will no longer tolerate his humiliating me in front of others. If he does not stop, I will leave the situation, even if it's a holiday function.

- *My partner:* I will no longer tolerate his demand for intimacy whenever he is in the mood when I am clearly not. I will leave or sleep in another room.

- *My coworker:* I will no longer tolerate her pushing off extra work to me because she is always in some crisis and behind in her work.

Make a plan to tell the people on your list in a compassionate way what your new boundaries are and ask them to respect them. Example:

- To a family member who always calls you at 10 p.m. to talk about her daily hassles, you might say this: *I know you have a lot going on right now in your life, and I want to hear about it, but I get up at 5 a.m. and I need to get to bed by ten. When you call me at ten and we talk for an hour, I don't get the sleep I require to function the next day. I am letting you know that from now on I won't answer my phone after 8 p.m. I hope you can respect this new time.*

Note: If friends do not accept or respect your new boundaries, consider letting them go. Find new friends who will respect your boundaries. With regard to family members, coworkers, or your boss—that is, people you can't just let go from your life or ignore—you can set tighter boundaries around them. For example, with family members, do not see them or talk on the phone as often, and if you do have to attend family functions, be polite and cordial but reserved. Stay only as long as necessary. With coworkers and bosses, be polite and professional. Politely decline their invitation to go to lunch or to have after-work cocktails with them. Focus on doing your work and avoid workplace gossip.

Acknowledge when others do respect your boundaries (this reinforces change). Examples:

- Thank someone who is being more respectful of your boundaries.

- Tell someone who is now respecting your boundaries how much happier it makes you or how it positively impacts your life.

- Let people know that you can see how they are trying to respect your boundaries.

Now that you've worked to make your boundaries healthier, let's take a look at your limits—recognizing how much you are capable of taking care of others while still taking care of yourself. In short, this means knowing when to say yes and when to say no to others.

Limits: Caring for Others and Caring for Yourself

Limits refer to knowing how much you are capable of doing for others while still taking care of yourself. You'll know how much you are capable of by paying attention to how you feel when you say yes to someone—for example, when you agree to go to the movies or dinner, volunteer for an event, or help someone move. If after you've said yes, you feel depressed, angry, or resentful, or have a knot in your stomach, that's a sure sign you really didn't want to do that particular thing. Why didn't you say no when you wanted to? The answer is you suffer from what has been called the "disease to please."

You need to learn how to say no. Think of saying no as saying yes to *you*—it's a form of self-care. It is taking care of you. But if you're afflicted with the disease to please, you probably feel guilty when you say no to someone. When a woman tells me she feels guilty saying no to someone, I ask her, "What was your intent when you said no?" Invariably, her response isn't that she wanted to disappoint, anger, or inconvenience someone. Therefore, if her intent wasn't to hurt another, she has nothing to feel guilty about. So, when we say no, the person to whom we say no may be disappointed, angry, or inconvenienced, but since our intent was not to make them feel that way, we have nothing to feel guilty about. What is usually difficult for people with the disease to please is that they don't like the way they feel when they think they've disappointed someone.

Saying no to someone's request is not about being selfish; it's about taking care of yourself. You may need to remind yourself that you do many things for others and that there are times that you will need to say no.

If you haven't done it before, it takes time to be comfortable with saying no and with setting limits on how much of yourself you'll share with someone—how much time or energy you can expend. But the more you practice limit setting, the more comfortable you will become. To help you become more comfortable, repeat the following to yourself every time you have to say no to someone: *I have the right to take care of myself and put my needs first. I am not responsible for another person's happiness. I cannot control how someone responds to my no.* The following exercise will also help you with limit setting.

Exercise 23: *What's My Limit?*

This exercise will help you identify your limits and provide tips for maintaining them. Begin by thinking about a situation when you said yes when you really wanted to say no. Record that situation in your journal. Then, carefully consider each item below and write your answers in your journal.

1. How did you feel when you said yes? Examples:
    *   Resentful
    *   Angry
    *   Sad
    *   Anxious
    *   Sick to my stomach
    *   Afraid
    *   Other response (be explicit)

2. Complete the following sentence and write it in your journal:

    The reason I couldn't say no was...

3. If you are caught off guard by someone's request, here are some ways to say no:
    *   I need to get back to you.
    *   I'll have to check my schedule.
    *   I need some time to think about that.

4. You don't need to justify your reason for saying no. Less is more: a simple no is often all you need to say. Examples:
    *   No, I'm sorry. I won't be able to do that.
    *   That time won't work for me.
    *   I can't make it that weekend.
    *   I'm not available then.
    *   I'm sorry; I realize I can't make it then.

5. Think again about the situation where you said yes when you really wanted to say no. How could you have said no? Think of two or three ways you could have said no. Write your responses in your journal.

6. If you had said no instead of yes, what would you have liked to have done in place of the activity/task you agreed to do? How would this have been a way of caring for yourself? Write your responses in your journal.

When you say no to someone's request of you, notice how you feel. You may feel guilty initially but then remember you have nothing to feel guilty about. Perhaps more important, be sure to notice how you feel when you are doing the thing you now get to do because you said no. Maybe you are taking care of something for yourself: running your errands, working out, reading, relaxing, gardening, or something else that nourishes you. Whatever it is, be sure to give yourself kudos for having the courage to say no and to take care of yourself. Remember that setting limits is like two oars moving a boat: learning when to say yes and when to say no will keep you moving toward taking care of yourself.

Now let's explore values. They will keep you aligned in the way that you want to think and behave, just as the rudder keeps a boat aligned in the desired direction.

Values

Values, like the rudder on a boat, keep you aligned with the things— such as family, commitment, health, and others—that mean the most to you. If you don't know what things are most important to you, you will be like a rudderless boat, drifting aimlessly. You will not know where you are going or what you are heading toward. Worse, you are at risk of being shanghaied by being forced to adhere to someone else's values.

Your values are unique and integral to who you are; they guide you in all aspects of your life. Who your friends are, what you do for a living, if you marry and who you marry, and on and on—your values impact every decision you make. Therefore, it is imperative you know what your values are.

Knowing your values will help you avoid repeating another relationship with a narcissist because a self-absorbed narcissist will not share values such as reciprocity, commitment, mutual respect, and so on. Too often women who get involved with a narcissistic partner ignore or minimize when the narcissist does not share their values. Some women may not even know what their values are because their childhood experiences taught them to ignore what's important to them.

Finding someone who matches up with your values is necessary for a healthy and lasting relationship. You don't have to have tons of similar interests, such as scuba diving or golf, but you do have to have shared values. For example, if you and your partner are from different religious backgrounds, say Catholic and Jewish, but you both share the value of family, you will work hard to have a wonderful family in spite of your religious differences. You will respect each other's religion and provide experiences in them both for your children, thus teaching them tolerance and respect for other's differences. You will also create a loving and wonderful family.

In order to help you know your values, I've compiled a list of twenty basic values, given in the exercise below. There are actually hundreds of values, but these are the most common and the ones I think are most important to have in order to avoid becoming involved with another narcissistic partner.

Exercise 24: *Rank Your Values*

Please read the list, and then rank each value according to which you value most or least (1 = most important, 2 = second most important, and so on). Feel free to add other values that are important to you that may not be listed.

_____ Commitment

_____ Communication or openness

_____ Dependability

_____ Family

_____ Financial stability

_____ Friendship

_____ Health

_____ Honesty

_____ Integrity

_____ Loyalty

_____ Professionalism

_____ Reliability

_____ Relationships

_____ Respect for self

_____ Respect for others

_____ Responsibility

_____ Religion or spirituality

_____ Service

_____ Stability

_____ Trustworthiness

_____ Other (write in journal)

Good job! Now let's look at which values you ranked highest and why. The next exercise will help you understand why certain values are most important to you. *Core values* are the ones that are most important to you, the ones you will not compromise; they are the deal breakers if someone does not share them with you, especially when dating. Recognizing that a potential partner does not share your core values can save you a lot of heartache later; you'll realize sooner that you need to move on to someone who does share your core values. If someone does not share your core values, end the relationship and move on.

Exercise 25: *What You Value Most*

In your journal, list your most important values, the five you ranked highest. These are your core values. Really think about why you hold these values. Write your thoughts in your journal. *Don't* worry if you haven't been living them. *Do* remember that your values keep you balanced by contributing to your sense of self and informing the limits of your behavior. I would even highlight or underline them: they are that important. Remind yourself of them often. A concrete way to do this is to write your core values on an index card or sticky note and post it somewhere you'll see it each day.

You're doing great work. You have identified your values and which are the most important to you—your core values. Doing this is important because knowing your values will help you make healthy decisions and act in healthy ways—in short, they'll help you take care of yourself. Now let's look at some other ways you can take care of yourself.

The next few exercises will help you learn to value yourself; they are part of a self-care regimen. Valuing yourself will help you to maintain your boundaries with others; you won't allow others (such as narcissists) to exploit you.

Exercise 26: *Be Kind to Yourself*

Demonstrate kindness and compassion toward yourself—and commit to doing at least one act of kindness toward yourself a day. Here is one way to start:

1. Think of seven acts of kindness that you can do toward or for yourself. Write them in your journal.

2. Cut up seven slips of paper—about the size of a business card—and write one act of kindness on each slip of paper and then fold it up.

3. Put the slips of paper in a container on your desk, by your bed, or some other place where you will see it.

4. For the next week, draw one slip of paper each day and do that act of kindness for yourself that day.

5. Repeat this exercise each week until being kind to yourself becomes a habit.

Exercise 27: *You Can Enjoy Being with Yourself*

Make a list of all the things you would typically only do with a date or partner—for example, go to the movies, a nice restaurant, a concert, an event, a retreat, or on a trip. Write this list in your journal. Now circle three items that you'd really like to do. Pull out your calendar and select a date on which you will do each item—and then do it!

Note: Feeling lonely is not the same as being alone. *Feeling lonely* is an emotional state of loss. There is a yearning for someone. *Being alone* is the state of being by oneself. It doesn't have to mean you feel loss and loneliness. Learn how to enjoy your own company. Spending time alone is an act of self-care and self-love. If you avoid being alone because it makes you feel lonely and creepy thoughts fill your mind—thoughts like *I'm alone because no one loves me* or *I don't have friends*—practice sitting alone with those thoughts and use realistic thinking (see chapter 6) to assess and evaluate each one of them rationally. Or practice mindful meditation and let your thoughts come and go. Try just sitting with your lonely thoughts and tolerating the feelings that come up. They are just thoughts and feelings and are probably distorted. If you find evidence for even one of them, make a plan for change using the six stages of behavioral change (see chapter 6). Don't wallow in them but take action. Use the skills in this chapter and chapter 6 to help you.

Exercise 28: *You Are Capable*

Make a list of all the things you might typically rely on a man to do, such as finances, car maintenance, yardwork, or home repairs. Be specific. For example, balance the checkbook, change the oil in the car, prune the rosebushes, or repair the leaky kitchen faucet. Write the list in your journal. Now circle three things that you'd really like to get done. Then make a plan to DIY! Here are some suggestions:

- Take a class on the basics of auto mechanics.

- Take a class in home repair. Local hardware stores will often put on workshops.

- Buy tools and a power drill. Learn how to use them.

- Find girlfriends who want to do these things with you.

Wow, you just learned a lot about how boundaries, limits, and values are part of taking care of yourself. Boundaries provide a barrier that protects you, like the hull protects the boat. Limits guide your behavior with others, like the oars guide the boat's movement. Values keep you aligned with the things that are most important to you, much like the rudder of a boat keeps the boat oriented in the desired direction.

When you demand that others respect your boundaries, when you can set limits and cure your disease to please, and when you know your values—what's most important to you—you are protecting and taking good care of yourself. Just like a fairy godmother would, you are watching over and protecting yourself.

Your Journey to Healing Through Self-Care

Healing is a journey—and healing from childhood wounds and relationships with narcissists can take a long time. But you've already come a long way on that journey since you started reading this book. You've learned skills and techniques, such as mindful breathing, mindful meditation, and realistic thinking (see chapter 6), that will help you change your life traps, which is a major step on the way to healing. In this chapter, you've learned several ways to care for yourself, all of which will contribute to your healing.

For healing to really take hold in your life, though, you'll need to practice these skills, techniques, and modes of self-care until they become second nature. Doing this may be difficult in the beginning because you're trying out new ways of behaving and of treating yourself, as well as new expectations of how others should treat you—with respect and honor. For now, practice these self-care skills in your relationships with friends, family, coworkers, and other acquaintances. You may wonder, *Why not my dates?* Well, right now, I hope you are *not* dating. You need to heal, you need to learn about yourself and really get these skills under your belt before you begin dating again. Please have patience. I know that many of you don't think you have the time to wait, but I promise that, if you date too soon out of fear of not having time, you will pick the wrong guy again. I don't want that to happen to you—and I know you don't want it to happen either. So, take your time now, practice these skills, and heal deeply so you will be ready to enter into a healthy relationship.

Putting It All Together

In this chapter, you learned self-care techniques, such as attending to the triad of wellness: nutrition, exercise, and sleep. You also learned about the importance of healthy boundaries, limits, and values. Boundaries provide a barrier that protects you from being used, manipulated, or exploited, like the hull protects a boat. Limits guide your behavior with others, how much you are capable of doing for another while still taking care of yourself, like the oars guide a boat's movement. Values keep you aligned with the things that are most important to you, the same way the rudder of a boat keeps the boat moving in the direction it's supposed to. Everything you learned in this chapter is built on treating yourself and expecting others to treat you with kindness, respect, and compassion. When you take care of yourself, you are being your own fairy godmother to the princess that is you.

The next chapter is about mindful dating. In it, you'll see how the skills and knowledge you have acquired in the previous chapters come together in an experience of healthy dating.

CHAPTER 8

Mindful Dating

This is the chapter you've been waiting for! All the hard work you've done throughout the book—completing exercises, reflecting on your relationships and life experiences, and delving into painful memories—has prepared you for a new kind of dating that I term "mindful dating." But what exactly does that mean and why is it important?

Mindful dating means holding an awareness of yourself—your life traps, core beliefs, coping styles, thoughts, feelings, values, boundaries, and limits—at the same time as you are assessing the person you're dating. Mindful dating is useful for anyone who dates, but it is absolutely imperative for women like you, who are determined not to have another relationship with a narcissist. Mindful dating helps you stay vigilant: you'll notice any of your date's behaviors that trigger your life traps or negative core beliefs, conflict with your values, or violate your boundaries or limits. This allows you to assess him and the situation realistically so you are able to recognize a narcissist and nip another unhealthy relationship in the bud.

Mindful dating encompasses not only the date, but the time before and after. To make the most of your dating learning curve, I recommend keeping track of your dating in a journal—or even keeping a separate journal that's just for dating. It is something you can refer back to to see your patterns and check your progress.

Now, it's possible that you still don't feel quite ready for dating mindfully, but I do know you long to be in a healthy romantic relationship. So, before we look more closely at the elements of mindful dating and healthy relationships, let's take a quick look at some of the things you've accomplished as you've worked through this book, all of which will help you make the dream of a healthy romantic relationship a reality.

Because of all the work you did in previous chapters, you have a stronger sense of self, which means that you know who you are and why you acted and thought in certain ways that unwittingly drew you toward narcissistic partners. You've also learned skills and techniques, such as mindful breathing, mindfulness meditation, and realistic thinking, to help you deal with your life traps and negative core beliefs. You've honed your self-care skills. Also, you now know that vulnerability can be a healthy openness in which you reveal your true self, an essential part of forging authentic relationships. Slowly, you've been building your courage to be yourself in a relationship with someone who truly wants to be in a relationship with the *real you*. So...to find that special relationship, you'll need to begin dating mindfully. If you still feel uncertain, that's okay. Pay attention to the timing that is right for you. Maybe you'll want some help as you move through this transition period. If you do, you may find working with a therapist helpful. Whatever you decide to do, trust what you've learned and how you've grown. Let's build on that a bit more as we explore mindful dating and healthy relationships more deeply.

Essential Elements

This chapter will describe what a healthy relationship—in other words, one that is reciprocal and trustworthy—looks like. You will learn how to assess if you are ready to start dating and if the person you choose to date is a healthy choice—not another narcissist. To help with this, we will cover red flags—things to watch out for on first dates and during a new relationship. You will learn how mindful dating incorporates everything you have learned to this point.

What Does a Healthy Relationship Look Like?

It is so easy to describe what an unhealthy romantic relationship looks like. Most of us have had one or more, but few of us have been lucky enough to have a healthy romantic relationship. We may even question if there is such a thing. If you have had a healthy relationship with someone, even if it wasn't a romantic one, you already know something about healthy relationships because all healthy relationships have the same traits. A healthy relationship includes *all* of these traits:

- mutual respect

- reciprocity

- commitment

- communication

- mutual trust

- healthy boundaries

- shared values

- flexibility

Let's take a closer look at each of these traits. Remember that *all of them are present in a healthy relationship.*

Mutual Respect

You acknowledge each other's opinions, even if they differ. You value and appreciate his opinion, and he values and appreciates yours. You treat each other as you would treat cherished friends. Always, even if you argue, you express your differences in a respectful manner. For example, you're talking with your date while eating dessert at a new restaurant you both wanted to try. He says he thought the restaurant was very good, but he was a little disappointed with his entrée. You are surprised and say you thought everything they served you tonight was terrific. He asks you why and you tell him what you liked about the food. He says this would not be his first choice of a restaurant, but if you like it that much he is willing to give it a second try. He smiles at you and you smile back. You finish your dessert, order a coffee, and talk about your plans for the next day.

Reciprocity

Give-and-take, or reciprocity, in a relationship is not about keeping score about who is doing what or doing more than the other. It is about mutually acknowledging that you and your partner are interdependent, meaning you each contribute to the relationship. You each take responsibility for the relationship and your role in it. For example, you are dating a guy who has ridiculously long work hours. You do, too. It's tough to find much time to be together. One night he calls you before you leave your workplace to ask if you want something from the take-out joint you like—he's offering to pick food up for dinner so the two of you can spend some time together. But this is the second time this week he's brought you take-out food. The following weekend you surprise him by inviting some of his friends over to barbecue and relax.

Commitment

You pledge responsibility to each other in good times and bad. Commitment to each other is the promise you share to be together. For example, let's say you have MS (multiple sclerosis) and can no longer work at your stressful marketing job. You and your partner discuss the impact on the household income and come up with a plan to work within your new budget.

Communication

Healthy communication means you both can discuss things in a mature way with mutual respect. You are open and honest with one another. In short, when one person speaks, the other listens—and vice versa. For example, if your date suggests you both spend Saturday watching your mutual college football game with his guy friends at a local sports bar and you would rather go to brunch and see the latest movie, you both listen to each other's concerns with respect. Maybe it goes something like this:

You: I understand you want to see the game, but I really
                          don't feel up to spending my Saturday afternoon in a

loud sports bar. I had a tough work week and I was looking forward to sleeping in and going to brunch, then maybe catching a movie.

Your partner: I had a tough work week, too, and my way of letting go of it is to have a few beers with the guys.

Having heard each other, you both might agree to have brunch together and then separate, so he can go watch the game with his friends and you go to your movie with a girlfriend. Or you might decide that you'll have brunch with a girlfriend while he goes to the game, and then the two of you would meet up later that evening for a movie.

Mutual Trust

Being able to be vulnerable with your partner requires mutual trust. You know he has your back, and you have his. You keep promises and commitments, which is something you both value and are committed to maintaining throughout the relationship. For example, when your partner makes a date with you for a certain night or to attend an event, he always follows through with his commitment. Or say you've been dating for a while and he invites you to his upcoming work party. You share that you get anxious at parties and meeting new people. At the party, he makes sure to stay by your side. When he introduces you to people, he points out something about you that fits in with the conversation, such as "You know, Sharon ran in the Chicago Marathon last year, too" or "Sharon also works in marketing for Blah Blah Corporation."

Healthy Boundaries

In a healthy relationship, you know and respect each other's boundaries. Healthy boundaries determine what you will or will not accept in terms of other people's behaviors or demands upon you. This is particularly important in an intimate relationship because you are either living together or spending much time together. For example, you ask permission to borrow his car. You don't just assume you can take it; this shows that you respect his boundary. Or, if he asks if he can come over and watch the Monday night football game at your house, you say, "You can come at halftime, because I have other plans and won't be home till then."

Shared Values

This is the glue that keeps you together. You can have differences of opinion, but if you have shared values, your relationship will survive. For example, while on a date, you learn he has a different religious background than yours but that he values family as you do. That shared value of family can transcend your religious differences if you both focus more on creating a strong, loving family than on which place of worship you attend.

Flexibility

As a couple, being open to change as well as allowing each other to explore and grow is important. This kind of flexibility and the growing and changing that come with it can stimulate a relationship. Flexibility also helps when couples face difficult challenges in their lives and relationship; it enables them to adapt as needed. For example, you're dating a guy you think is terrific. Together you made plans to attend the wedding of his best friend, but now you need to cancel. You've just learned about an important business conference you need to attend, which is scheduled for the same weekend. He is disappointed but recognizes you can't miss this business opportunity. When you see each other the following week, after the wedding and business conference, you are both eager to share stories from your respective weekends.

Your Looking Glass

Reflect on your most significant romantic relationships. Using the list of healthy relationship traits above, assess each of your significant relationships and count how many healthy traits each one had.

Look for patterns. For example, perhaps most of your romantic relationships had relatively good communication and commitment, but you did not share core values. Note honestly which traits were yours, which were your partner's, and which were shared. Record these findings in your journal. These reflections will give you a better understanding of what healthy traits you keep missing in men. In other words, which traits weren't present in your previous relationships? Now look for someone who embodies all of the traits.

How Do You Know When It's Time to Start Dating?

I believe you are ready to date when you feel confident that you understand the part you played in repeating your narcissistic relationships. Such understanding involves being aware of your life traps, knowing your values, having a plan for and commitment to self-care, and developing a healthy sense of self-love and self-appreciation. There is no prescribed time as to when to start dating. You must do an individual assessment of your own preparedness, though I urge you not to date too soon after ending a relationship with a narcissist. Having a deeper understanding of yourself will help you feel more confident in connecting with another.

If you do feel confident, first explore your motivation for dating. Here are some common reasons women cite for dating; if these are your reasons for dating, you may be vulnerable to "settling" for a narcissist:

- My biological clock is ticking.

- I feel left behind because all my friends have boyfriends or are married.

- I'm lonely.

- I'm afraid to be alone.

- I want to start my life.

- I will be happy if I meet someone.

These reasons are more likely to lead you toward a healthy partner:

- I feel reasonably confident in myself.

- I recognize and appreciate what I have to offer another person.

- I value myself and know my self-worth.

- I have a healthy level of self-awareness and insight into my issues and vulnerabilities and am ready to find a partner who has the same.

- I have given myself the time and space to heal the wounds from previous destructive relationships and will not be carrying this hurt and resentment into my next relationship.

The quality of your relationship with yourself will determine the quality of your relationship with another. If you do not value yourself and do not love yourself, you will not attract a healthy partner. When you value yourself, you will make better dating choices. You will recognize healthy partners and will not accept being treated any other way than with respect.

When you feel ready to date, I suggest that you not limit yourself only to men you think are candidates for Mr. Right, meaning candidates for marriage or men with whom you want to have a long-term relationship. It can be valuable to practice your skills and gain confidence with Mr. Right Now, providing he is a healthy candidate. Sometimes Mr. Right Now can become Mr. Right. I have known many women who declined a second date with a nice man because he was, in their opinion, boring or not inter-esting enough, when in actuality, they were still caught up in the fantasy that their ideal date would be exciting and sweep them off their feet. But in some cases, with encouragement in therapy to try a second or third date, they came to appreciate their date, and for some of them, he turned into a partner.

Right now, your dating goal is to distinguish the healthy men from the narcissists. I'm talking about dating casually so you can both practice the skills you've learned as you've worked your way through this book and draw on what you have learned about yourself up to now. If you are concerned about misleading a nice guy who is looking for a long-term relationship, be honest: tell him that you are just reentering the world of dating after a hiatus and are not looking for a serious relationship. And if you happen to meet a really nice guy you'd like to see again, great. A lot of people do "light" dating just for fun and to get out and meet people. Each person you spend time with will help you learn more about yourself and will help you practice setting boundaries, speaking your mind, and expecting respect.

By the same token, taking this approach of dating casually and carefully when reentering the world of dating will also help you be less focused on "the man of your dreams" and more focused on "the self of your dreams." At first, this may sound selfish, but remember, the more you know and love yourself, the more likely you will attract a healthy partner who also loves and knows himself.

Your Looking Glass

Using the checklist below, assess how ready you are to date. Use the following scale to score yourself: Unsatisfactory (1), Needs Improvement (2), Fair (3), Good (4), Excellent (5). Write your score in the blank next to each category.

Dating Readiness Checklist

_____ Self-Care

- Nutrition
- Exercise
- Sleep

_____ Relaxation

- Mindfulness meditation—formal
- Mindfulness meditation—informal
- Mindful breathing

_____ Boundaries
- Emotional
- Psychological
- Physical
- Sexual
- Spiritual

_____ Limits
- How good am I at saying no?
- Do I take care of myself when I am doing things for others?

_____ My Values
- How well do I know them?
- How well do I adhere to them?

_____ Shame and Vulnerability
- Have I shared the things I am most ashamed of with another?
- Do I have the courage to take the risk to be vulnerable?

_____ Support System
- Trusted friends
- Family
- Therapist

After you have scored the checklist above, write in your journal an action step to address each one. You can use the six stages of change and/or realistic thinking (see chapter 6) to help you.

You have learned that narcissists are masters at presenting themselves well, and they can fool even the best of us. Because of this, the next section names the red flags, specific to narcissists, to watch out for when dating.

What Are the Red Flags?

Identifying red flags early in the dating process, or at any time in the relationship, can save you heartache later. This is particularly true when you're trying to avoid another relationship with a narcissist. Too often we focus on having our date like us rather than on assessing him accurately. If your goal is to find a long-term, healthy, satisfying relationship, you may miss or ignore red flags waving right in front of you. You know that narcissists often present themselves really well, and you also know you are susceptible to this type of man, so you must be especially vigilant to red flags.

Also, as you date a person, remember that a narcissist may not show his true self for a while, so don't rush to judgment, deciding quickly that he is a wonderful guy. Give yourself adequate time to make an accurate assessment. But if any of the red flags I offer below do come up, please do not dismiss them as "not that bad" or an anomaly.

Even if you're enjoying an exchange, does he monopolize the conversation? Does he listen to you? Is the conversation give-and-take?

Narcissists are known for holding court. Even if they aren't talking about themselves, they are probably the only ones talking. They just like to hear themselves talk. It's as if they never learned the art of conversation, where you talk a bit, pause, and allow another to speak. And, if you don't try to speak up, he'll just keep going.

Does he ask questions about you? Does he demonstrate interest in you?

Narcissists are not interested in others, except for what others can do for them. So if you are in conversation with a narcissist, it is because he wanted you to be there as his audience. For example, one woman told me her date never asked one question about her the entire night. If you happen to hold a position of prestige, he may ask questions that indicate interest in you, but his true motive will be to win you over because he finds value in being associated with you. In another situation, the narcissist did ask questions of the woman, but they were all about the work they were collaborating on and not really about her, who she was, what she liked, or what she was about. Again, the woman was providing something the narcissist wanted or needed. It can be easy to misinterpret this kind of interest as something more. If you are involved with this type of narcissist intimately, you may not realize that he is only with you as long as you have something to offer him. Once you don't, he can drop you fast—and feel nothing about it.

Does he mostly talk about himself?

If this is the case, check to see if he is just nervous by interjecting something about yourself and see how he responds. If he glosses over it and brings the conversation back to himself, you have your answer.

If you continue to date, does he only suggest things he likes to do, or does he try to do things you like as well?

If it seems as though your partner is just fitting you into his life and not accommodating your interests, that is a red flag. One woman told me her date would only go to a particular type of restaurant, even though she repeatedly told him she wanted to go elsewhere. He also only took her to sporting events and movies he liked.

Is he too agreeable?

Beware of a man who is too quick to change his wishes to accommodate you. Don't be fooled into thinking how wonderful he is because he likes everything you do. This may be the chameleon narcissist who is doing and saying whatever he can to snare you. Also, I would have concerns if your date agrees with everything you say or do. He may expect something from you in return for all his agreeableness. Then, if he doesn't get what he wants, he may sulk, pout, or—worse—say you're ungrateful after all he has done for you. In other words, everything he did for you was conditional.

Does he easily become defensive?

Does he become defensive when you ask questions? Does he become defensive when you ask follow-up questions in an effort to clarify something or if you challenge him on a topic?

Are his answers to your questions vague or fantastical?

When he does answer questions, are you left unclear as to his answer? For example, you ask about where he grew up and he says the Midwest. You ask where and he says all over. You tell yourself, *Maybe he is just private."* Maybe—but pay attention. If all his answers are vague, it may indicate he is hiding something or needs to control situations. One woman's date told her a fantastic tale about working for the CIA on a secret mission while he was in college. This is a clear case of needing to pay attention to a red flag.

Is he unable to laugh at himself?

Narcissists can have a sense of humor but rarely about themselves. They tend to take themselves very seriously. Since their ego is so fragile, they cannot tolerate anyone poking fun at them. They don't typically laugh at their own foibles because that would acknowledge that they are, indeed, flawed, just like the rest of us.

Is he hypercritical of others—or of you?

Pay attention to if and how he criticizes or puts others down or speaks of others with contempt. It may indicate how he will be with you in the future. If he is critical of you but masks it as playful teasing, pay attention. Sometimes teasing can be thinly veiled hostility. How you feel in these situations will help you determine whether it's teasing or hostility. Also, if you ask him not to tease you about something and he continues to do so, you'll know he does not respect you—a red flag.

Is he quick to anger?

Does he always complain about how others are idiots, or about how no one really gets him or appreciates him at work or in his family? Does he overreact to seemingly innocent situations? For example, if the teen movie attendant gives him the wrong change, does he get angry and berate the kid, pummeling him with words? In short, is he a hothead?

Is he able to apologize if he makes a mistake?

Because narcissists believe they never do anything wrong or make a mistake, they don't think they have any reason to apologize. They often don't even realize they have made a mistake, and if you point it out to them, they may attack you by pointing out a mistake you once made. But if someone you date *is* able to apologize, ask yourself if the apology is sincere and genuine. Then observe him over time to see if he is able to own his mistakes.

Does he lack boundaries?

There are all kinds of boundaries, but pay close attention to the emotional and physical ones. As an example of emotional boundary violations, he might ask you personal, maybe even inappropriate, questions or become too familiar too soon. One woman told me that early in a first date, the man started addressing her as "Hon." Terms of endearment, like this one, take time to develop and are based on a true relationship; they are not appropriate for a first date. You'll know when your date crosses an emotional boundary because you will feel uncomfortable.

And then there are violations of physical boundaries. Here's a good example from real life. I worked with a woman who brought a guy home for coffee on their first date. The first thing he did, without asking, was open her refrigerator. Now, you may think that is a small thing, as she did. I, however, did not. I expressed my concern that he was not respecting her boundaries and that this was a huge red flag, but she dated him anyway. Six months later he broke her heart with nary a care—when she no longer served a purpose for him, he dumped her. She was devastated. Would you walk into a stranger's house for the first time and open the refrigerator, under any circumstances? No. So why make excuses for him, like "I am so glad he feels comfortable enough to feel at home in my house"?

Does he overwhelm you with fast chemistry?

Too often I hear women say things like "He swept me off my feet" or "I feel like he's a soul mate" or "No one has ever understood me like this before." When this happens right away, it's always a red flag. Narcissists are notorious for making you feel like this. Proceed with caution. It feels great to have strong chemistry with someone. That electrifying feeling can be intoxicating, but it also can be a red flag. Be extra careful if you hear yourself saying that he is perfect! And if you find yourself almost giddy in love, catch yourself. Remember, you're a grown, mature, intelligent woman. Don't let him sweet-talk you about how he has never felt this way with anyone—and be careful not to say things like that to him. If you use terms like "soul mate" right away after a first date, just be cautious.

Does he boast about how he gets away with things, and how clever he is at bending the rules and not getting caught?

Narcissists feel they are not bound by the same rules as everyone else. After all, they are special. Also, they pride themselves on being clever enough to get away with things. A woman I worked with reported meeting a guy while on vacation at a tropical island. He told her that he was there on business but was sneaking off in a couple days because he knew how to trick his office so they would never know. If he lies to others, it's likely just a matter of time until he lies to you. Red flag!

Finally, are your own thoughts or expectations sending you red flags?

If you don't like something about him but think to yourself, *Oh, he'll change later,* watch out. I have seen too many women who thought this way about a partner who didn't want children or who didn't share their values. If he tells you he does not want children, do not tell yourself he will change in time. He might, but you may be setting yourself up for heartache. Even if he is on the fence about children, do not assume it means he will come over to your side. He may not. Do you really want to invest your time in a fifty-fifty possibility? It may be better to cut the ties and find someone who shares your values of children and family outright. The point is to pay attention to your own thoughts and reactions.

When you see one of these red flags, don't make a snap judgment, automatically eliminating this man from your life. However, be cautious. Know that if you see these traits at any time, he may not be worth pursuing.

Now that you know the red flags, let's explore what it means to date mindfully. By dating with awareness, you'll be able to avoid another relationship with a narcissist. Not only that, you may be on your way to finding Mr. Right.

How to Date Mindfully

We've covered a lot of territory since the beginning of the chapter, so let me offer a little refresher on what mindful dating is. When you date mindfully, you are fully aware of both yourself and your date. You're aware of your life traps, core beliefs, boundaries, limits, and values, as well as your thoughts and feelings; you're also aware of any of your date's behaviors that trigger your life traps or negative core beliefs, conflict with your values, or violate your boundaries or limits. This awareness allows you to assess your date to see if he is a narcissist or not as well as to assess the potential for a healthy relationship with him.

During mindful dating, practice your self-care techniques. You will be better prepared to date if you feel mentally and physically healthy and strong, so be sure you are eating well, exercising, and getting enough sleep. Also, continue to practice mindful meditation—formal and informal—as well as mindful breathing, and maintain your support group of trusted people. The exercise below will help you as you enter the world of mindful dating.

Exercise 29: *Keeping a Dating Journal*

Buy yourself a new notebook to use as your dating journal; a new notebook is symbolic of your new life. (Or, if you prefer, you can use your regular journal.) Use the sections below to grow mindfully through dating.

A Declaration of Intent
On the first page of your dating journal, write something that speaks to your commitment to yourself, such as "I will never be disrespected again" or "No more narcissists!" or whatever you feel declares your intent to stay narcissist free. Underneath your declaration, write the one affirmation that best reflects your commitment to change. This first page is what you will look at before every date. Don't just look at it, but feel it, breathe it, and integrate it into your being. You will gain emotional strength from it.

Your Core Being
In this section, write down those fundamental elements that make up your core being: your life traps, your core beliefs, and coping styles that you tend to use. This will remind you to keep these at

the forefront of your mind so you can catch yourself when they get triggered or activated. Write down the triggers that make you most vulnerable. You want to always be mindful of them so you can protect yourself. Knowing your triggers and how you might respond to them will be invaluable to you as you date. Remember, a narcissist is really good at making you feel good and special in the beginning. This can be very disarming.

Also, remind yourself of your boundaries and limits: your boundaries determine what you will or will not accept in terms of other people's behaviors or demands upon you; and your limits are about knowing when to say no; they are a form of self-care.

Values

Next, list your core values, which you determined in chapter 6. These will serve as your rudder, guiding you in the direction of what's most important to you. On a first date and in every encounter afterward, you want to be clear about your values and observe how they compare to your new partner's values.

Questions to Consider Before Going on a Date

Take some time to record your answers to the following questions in your dating journal:

- *What is my motivation for going out with this person?* Take the time to explore why you said yes to him or why you asked him out on a date.

- *What are my expectations?* Write them down. Are they realistic? For example, are you fantasizing about a future with this man and you have not even had a first date with him? You want to hold reasonable expectations. For example, remind yourself that this is just one date and your whole future happiness is not contingent on it. Tell yourself, *I will learn more about this man on this date. That will inform me if I want to continue to get to know him after tonight. I am the selector, not just a selectee.*

- *How do I feel?* Are you anxious, scared, elated, worried? Explore why and write it down. If you are anxious or scared, remind and reassure yourself that you are prepared for this date and that you have something to offer. Again, you are the selector. If you are excited or elated, check out your reason for feeling this way and be sure you are not having unrealistic romantic notions about him. That is a surefire way to give the reins over to a narcissist. If possible, it's best to feel as neutral as possible, though you can be cautiously optimistic. See it as an adventure, an opportunity to try out your newly learned skills. You cannot lose. Even if the date is a bust, you will learn something from it. Every encounter with another offers that.

- *Am I having fantasies about how to please him, but I'm not being my authentic self?* This is where knowing your life traps, core beliefs, and triggers is so critical. If you go on a date and are only thinking about how important it is to get to the second date, are you being yourself?

Before each date, review your values, and remind yourself of the things that trigger your life traps, core beliefs, and coping styles. Know the way you will handle yourself if you are triggered. What healthy coping styles can you practice? For example, you can take a time-out, breathe, recall your values, remember your declaration of intent, or escape to call a trusted friend who can help you stay focused.

Questions to Ask Yourself While on a Date

The acronym OBSERVE will serve you well. I encourage you to memorize and practice it while on your date.

- **O**bserve him and observe your own feelings. If you are uncomfortable, is he making you feel this way?

- **B**reathe: Breathe naturally. If you find you are breathing rapidly, try to take some deep breaths—breathe mindfully.

You can excuse yourself to go to the ladies' room and take five to ten deep breaths.

- **S**elf: Check in with yourself to see how you are feeling. Trust your gut.

- **E**xpectations: Pay attention to any expectations that come up. See how realistic they are.

- **R**ed flags: Watch for them.

- **V**alues: Keep them present and on your mind.

- **E**njoy yourself. Remember this is supposed to be an enjoyable time, not drudgery.

Questions to Ask Yourself After a Date

Either right after your date or as soon as you can, do an honest dating assessment: What went well and what did not? Write down any red flags, or if you noticed your comfort level change during your time together. Take the time to explore each of these questions: How did you feel while on the date? Given how you handled this date, what would you want to change about the way you handle things next time? Does this person have friends? How is he perceived by his friends, coworkers, and family members? If you feel he is your soul mate, what are your shared values? How do you know those are his values? Because he told you? Now you have to take time to see if he can walk the walk, not just talk the talk. If you like him and want to go on a second date, do so, but remember it may take numerous dates or even months to really see him. Talk to a trusted friend about the date and ask her for her feelings and feedback. Try to listen with an open mind, without getting defensive.

Keeping a dating journal may feel cumbersome at first, but it's important because it keeps you grounded and on track. Otherwise, you will miss the red flags. Too often we don't want to see the truth, but only what we want to see. It's a fact. Answering these questions in your journal may help you see the whole picture, not just want you want to see. Hopefully, this will help you avoid being heartbroken again.

Think of mindful dating and all the effort you are putting into doing it as an investment in yourself. All your hard work will pay off: think of how good it will feel when you meet someone who treats you with respect, shares your values, and accepts you as the unique woman you are. Remember, mindful dating is not only a way out of repeating narcissistic relationships but also a way into a healthy relationship, the kind you deeply desire.

Putting It All Together

Hopefully, you are now well aware of the truth that when you authentically care for and respect yourself, you are able to recognize a narcissist and nip a potentially unhealthy relationship in the bud. Practice mindful dating. Take your time and go slow when dating. Pay attention to how you feel and how he makes you feel. Accept and acknowledge that you are fragile when you start to date again. Remember, the goal is to have a healthy relationship that will last, not just a relationship that fails again. Doing so becomes much less challenging and far more instinctive when you make this genuine commitment: *No more narcissists!*

A Few Last Thoughts...

Congratulations! You've completed *No More Narcissists!*—you've read the book all the way through, done the exercises, and learned a lot of really important things about yourself. The fact that you hung in there, even when you encountered difficult memories and relived painful experiences, means that you take changing your life seriously. I am impressed with your commitment to yourself and to change, because change takes courage— and that means *you* have courage.

This book has always been about *you*, not the narcissist. I hope you have learned that it was never your fault that you were repeatedly attracted to narcissists, but rather it was the result of your childhood beliefs that you carried unwittingly into adulthood. Your awareness of yourself, which has increased as you've worked through this book, will help you break your pattern of repeating relationships with narcissists. You've learned skills to help you as you change—as you leave behind relationships with narcis-sistic men and move toward healthy romantic relationships.

Be gentle with yourself during this time of change. Remember that we can only learn from our experiences, so if you find yourself slipping back, remember the stages of change. Don't worry, though, because you will gain insight from whatever experiences you go through, and it is only through experience that you learn and change. Sometimes we have to learn something over and over again before it really sticks.

Remember that you can come back to this book as often as you need. Maybe read through it again and even do the exercises again. If you do, you will probably have different answers the next time you do it as you continue to grow. These ideas and concepts are timeless, so check in again and again with yourself. It is my sincere wish that this book will be like an old friend you can come back to any time you need. I know it's not easy to do this work, and it takes courage and time to change. It is a process, and sometimes it's two steps forward and one step back. But you are heading in the right direction: toward a healthy relationship. With time, practicing the skills you've learned in this book and living your life more authentically will become more natural. It takes time and commitment, but I know you can do it. Along with the countless other women I have worked with over the years, you *will* get there!

Acknowledgments

I must thank all of the wonderful women I have been privileged to work with over the years who let me into their lives and shared their experiences with me. It is through your stories of struggle and redemption that other women may benefit. I am forever in awe of your strength and courage. I respect you all immensely.

A huge thank-you goes to my new family, New Harbinger Publications. Thank you for taking a chance on an unknown author and for your commitment to bringing books that truly help people to publication:

To my angel, Wendy Millstine, my acquisitions editor at New Harbinger. The universe perceptively placed us at the same conference, in the same lecture, seated next to one another. I am forever indebted to you for being interested in my book idea and believing in this project. You were instrumental in getting my book accepted, and your efforts launched me on this amazing journey of writing a book.

To Melissa Valentine, acquisitions editor, and Nicola Skidmore, associate editor. Your guidance and expertise provided me with constructive criticism to make this the best book it could be.

To the art department, and especially Amy Shoup, art director. Your dazzling cover design for the book exceeded my expectations!

To Clancy Drake, editorial manager; Fiona Hannigan, marketing and publicity associate; Cassie Kolias, publicist; and all the others at New Harbinger who brought this book into being. So many people have been involved in publishing this book, including many I've never met or had contact with, but I'm grateful to you all. Thank you!

I also want to thank Jeanne Ballew, my extraordinarily gifted writing coach and editor. Using your unique coaching process, you helped me figure out my structure and content, never losing sight of my intent or vision. You provided endless encouragement and gave me the confidence to find my voice and stay true to it. Without you, Jeanne, I wouldn't have a book.

To Jean M. Blomquist, the immensely gifted copy editor who edited my manuscript. Your insight, brilliant suggestions, and eye that never missed one detail truly brought this book to a new level. I am so grateful for all your gifts. And thank you for your patience when I needed to vent.

A special thanks to those who helped me at the very beginning of the writing process, when I was completely terrified and lost:

To my old friend Jared How, a wonderful writer, for helping me through those first months of agonizing self-doubt. Your patience, support, and editing were invaluable.

To my brother, Dean Melonas, who took time out of his very busy schedule to read my early writing and provide me with much needed feedback. I thank you.

To Laura Golden Belotti and Kate Zendall, two remarkable writers and editors I had the pleasure of working with at the beginning of this process. My thanks to you.

To my personal cheerleader and cousin, Jeanie Sears, who is like a sister to me. Your unending emotional support provided me with a constant source of encouragement that helped me through those dark days of writing when I was discouraged and doubting myself.

And finally, I would like to thank Carrol Stovold, licensed clinical social worker and, luckily for me, Reiki master. The energy from your warm, gentle hands soothed and grounded me during the early days of the writing process.

Appendix: List of Exercises

Chapter 1—Prince Charming or Another Frog?

Exercise 1: Your Core Beliefs

Exercise 2: Your Life Traps Associated with Narcissistic Partners

Chapter 2—The Frog: Understanding Narcissism and Narcissists

Exercise 3: Identify Your Narcissistic Partners

Chapter 4—A Closer Look at Life Traps

Exercise 4: Origins of Your Childhood Life Traps

Exercise 5: Write a Childhood Narrative

Exercise 6: Key Words

Exercise 7: Complete the Sentence

Chapter 5—Stuck for Life? Your Life Traps in Adulthood

Exercise 8: Which Life Traps Are Still at Play Within You?

Exercise 9: Key Words

Exercise 10: Complete the Sentence

Chapter 6—Learn to Change Your Life Traps

Exercise 11: Changing a Behavior

Exercise 12: Mindful Breathing

Exercise 13: Formal Mindfulness Meditation

Exercise 14: Informal Mindfulness

Exercise 15: Realistic Thinking

Chapter 7—Self-Care: Becoming Your Own Fairy Godmother

Exercise 16: Mindful Nutrition

Exercise 17: Mindful Eating

Exercise 18: Commit to Be Fit

Exercise 19: Sweet Dreams

Exercise 20: Finding Your Safe Place

Exercise 21: A Way to Sleep: Visualizing Your Safe Place

Exercise 22: Create Healthy Boundaries

Exercise 23: What's My Limit?

Exercise 24: Rank Your Values

Exercise 25: What You Value Most

Exercise 26: Be Kind to Yourself

Exercise 27: You Can Enjoy Being with Yourself

Exercise 28: You Are Capable

Chapter 8—Mindful Dating

Exercise 29: Keeping a Dating Journal

Notes

1   J. E. Young and J. S. Klosko, *Reinventing Your Life: The Breakthrough Program to End Negative Behavior...and Feel Great Again* (New York: Penguin Group, 1994).

2   Young and Klosko, *Reinventing Your Life.*

3   C. Diaz, K. Winslet, J. Law, et al., *The Holiday* (DVD), *directed by Nancy Meyers* (Culver City, CA: Columbia Pictures, 2006).

4   American Psychiatric Association, *Diagnostic and Statistical Manual of Mental Disorders*, 5th ed. (Arlington, VA: American Psychiatric Association, 2013).

5   W. T. Behary, *Disarming the Narcissist*, 2nd ed. (Oakland, CA: New Harbinger Publications, 2013).

6   E. D. Payson, *The Wizard of Oz and Other Narcissists* (Royal Oak, MI: Julian Day Publications, 2002).

7   Payson, *The Wizard of Oz and Other Narcissists*, 17.

8   Payson, *The Wizard of Oz and Other Narcissists*, 17.

9   American Psychiatric Association, *DSM-5.*

10 B. Brown, *Daring Greatly: How the Courage to Be Vulnerable Transforms the Way We Live, Love, Parent, and Lead* (New York: Penguin Group, 2012).

11 Brown, *Daring Greatly*, 71.

12 Brown, *Daring Greatly*.

13 B. Brown, *The Gifts of Imperfection: Let Go of Who You Think You're Supposed to Be and Embrace Who You Are* (Center City, MN: Hazelden Foundation), 6.

14 W. T. Behary, *Disarming the Narcissist* (Oakland, CA: New Harbinger Publications, 2013).

15 M. Beattie, *Codependent No More: How to Stop Controlling Others and Start Caring for Yourself* (Center City, MN: Hazelden Foundation, 1992), 33, my emphasis.

16 J. O. Prochaska, J. C. Norcross, and C. C. DiClemente, *Changing for Good: A Revolutionary Six-Stage Program for Overcoming Bad Habits and Moving Your Life Positively Forward* (New York: HarperCollins Publishers, 2010).

17 B. Stahl and E. Goldstein, *A Mindfulness-Based Stress Reduction Workbook* (Oakland, CA: New Harbinger Publications, 2010).

18 Mayo Clinic Staff, "Complications," April 4, 2014, http://www.mayo clinic.org/diseases-conditions/insomnia/basics/complications/con -20024293.

19 Jared D. Minkel, Siobhan Banks, O. Htaik, et al., "Sleep Deprivation and Stressors: Evidence for Elevated Negative Affect in Response to Mild Stressors When Sleep Deprived," *Emotion* 5: 1015–20.

20 American Psychiatric Association, *DSM-V*, 368.

References

American Psychiatric Association. 2013. *Diagnostic and Statistical Manual of Mental Disorders.* 5th ed. Arlington, VA: American Psychiatric Association.

Beattie, M. 1992. *Codependent No More: How to Stop Controlling Others and Start Caring for Yourself.* Center City, MN: Hazelden Foundation.

Behary, W. T. 2013. *Disarming the Narcissist.* Oakland, CA: New Harbinger Publications.

Brown, B. 2010. *The Gifts of Imperfection: Let Go of Who You Think You're Supposed to Be and Embrace Who You Are.* Center City, MN: Hazelden Foundation.

Brown, B. 2012. *Daring Greatly: How the Courage to Be Vulnerable Transforms the Way We Live, Love, Parent, and Lead.* New York: Penguin Group.

Diaz, C., K. Winslet, J. Law, et al. 2006. *The Holiday.* DVD. Directed by Nancy Meyers. Culver City, CA: Columbia Pictures.

Mayo Clinic Staff. 2014. "Complications." April 4, 2014. http://www.mayo clinic.org/diseases-conditions/insomnia/basics/complications/con -20024293.

Minkel, Jared D., Siobhan Banks, O. Htaik, Marisa C. Moreta, Christopher W. Jones, Eleanor L. McGlinchey, Norah S. Simpson, and David F. Dinges. 2012. "Sleep Deprivation and Stressors: Evidence for Elevated Negative Affect in Response to Mild Stressors When Sleep Deprived." *Emotion* 5: 1015–20.

Payson, E. D. 2002. *The Wizard of Oz and Other Narcissists*. Royal Oak, MI: Julian Day Publications.

Prochaska, J. O., J. C. Norcross, and C. C. DiClemente. 2010. *Changing for Good: A Revolutionary Six-Stage Program for Overcoming Bad Habits and Moving Your Life Positively Forward*. New York: HarperCollins Publishers.

Stahl, B., and E. Goldstein. 2010. *A Mindfulness-Based Stress Reduction Workbook*. Oakland, CA: New Harbinger Publications.

Young, J. E. 2003. *Schema Therapy: A Practitioner's Guide*. New York: Guilford Press.

Young, J. E., and J. S. Klosko. 1994. *Reinventing Your Life: The Breakthrough Program to End Negative Behavior...and Feel Great Again*. New York: Penguin Group.

As a licensed clinical psychologist, **Candace V. Love, PhD**, is passionate about helping women avoid narcissistic relationships. As founder and president of North Shore Behavioral Medicine, which has offices in downtown Chicago and Grayslake, IL, Love uses evidence-based techniques derived from cognitive behavioral therapies, including mindfulness and schema therapy. Much of her spare time is divided between the least narcissistic of creatures—namely animals. She enjoys riding horses and rehabilitating feral cats in the woods behind her home, and indulging in the next foodie find—whether it be a gourmet meal, vintage wine, or craft beer.

MORE BOOKS *from*
NEW HARBINGER PUBLICATIONS

Register your **new harbinger** titles for additional benefits!

When you register your **new harbinger** title—purchased in any format, from any source—you get access to benefits like the following:

- Downloadable accessories like printable worksheets and extra content
- Instructional videos and audio files
- Information about updates, corrections, and new editions

Not every title has accessories, but we're adding new material all the time.

Access free accessories in 3 easy steps:

1. Sign in at NewHarbinger.com (or **register** to create an account).

2. Click on **register a book**. Search for your title and click the **register** button when it appears.

3. Click on the **book cover or title** to go to its details page. Click on **accessories** to view and access files.

That's all there is to it!

If you need help, visit:

NewHarbinger.com/accessories

new harbinger
CELEBRATING
40 YEARS